You Only Live Until You Die

You Only Live Until You Die

by

Sol Weinstein

Combustoica
a prose project of About Comics - Camarillo, California

THE CHARACTERS, PLACES AND EVENTS IN THIS
MASTERWORK ARE WHOLLY FICTIONAL. ANY RESEMBLANCE,
BY NAME OR OTHERWISE, TO PERSONS LIVING OR DEAD,
ABOUT TO BE CONCEIVED, ABOUT TO BE BORN OR ABOUT TO
DIE IS PURELY COINCIDENTAL.

You Only Live Until You Die
By Sol Weinstein

This edition has been reedited by the original author from his
1968 novel.

Published by Combustoica, a prose project of About Comics.
WWW.COMBUSTOICA.COM

Rights inquiries? *rights@AboutComics.com*

Dedications

RONNIE AXE
In Memoriam.

SAM and CHAI SOORA WEINSTEIN, ELLIE, DAVID and JUDY WEINSTEIN, DR. and MRS. HOWARD FRIEDMAN, HARRY and BESS EISNER, STAN and RHODA EISNER, JOE E. LEWIS, DON and SANDY BARNETT, JACKIE (RATFINK ROOM) GANNON, LOUIE and CAROLE KAMER, WALT and MATTI MYERS, BEVERLEY GITHENS, LAURA LANE, SANDY LESBERG, DR. HERMAN CORN, DR. JULIUS SOBEL, IDA BLITMAN BOB BOOKER and GEORGE FOSTER, LOU JACOBI, MARJORIE RUTH BERNSTEIN, LINDA LATZ, SHIRLEY TABACKMAN, ART HOPPE, BOB and VICKI LANE. DICK and ANDY MATHEWS, HERBERT EDELMAN, SAM JACOBS, MRS. E. LAUREN HOWIE TEDDER, BOB TEDDER, WARREN RENSHAW, ALPHA EPSILON PI of EMORY U. and RABBI HERBERT HENDEL.

MR and MRS. I. (DICK) AXE, CAROLE AXE, MORT SLAKOFF, BILL LEWIS, AUSTIN MACK HANNAH GRATZ, JAMES R. LOWELL, MAX LERNER, ROSARA BERMAN, MRS. ABRAHAM E. WEINBERG, ETTA KLEINER, BILLY GARBER, JEFF KELLER, JOAN KARPINSKI, MARCELLA TRUDNAK, MR. and MRS. SID LUTZKER, TED and SYBIL COOPER, LEN and HELENA BOGARDE, DENIS P. DORSEY, LAWRENCE OKAMURA, LEO RUTKOFF, JACK and MARY SHERMAN, JACK and DORIS SHERMAN, JOSH SHERMAN, HARRY and JOHN HOLLAND, IRWIN and MARGIE WEINSTEIN JOHNNY COATES JR., JOHNNY COATES SR., BOB (SMOKEY) STOVER, IRWIN MOSES, ART SHAINES, JERRY NEELMAN, FRANK SADOFSKY, JAMES M. STILL JR., MARVIN and BERNIE BLUMENTHAL, HERB and SAM BLUMENTHAL, DANNY ROTH, BEN MELZER, STAN LEDERMAN, NEWMAN HOFFMAN, GEORGE GORDON, PAULA MELZER, JULIA HECKEL, MARILYNN FULTON and DR. BERNIE AMSTER.

EARL WILSON, SAMMY DAVIS, KARL BARRIE, MORTY GUNTY, LEE TULLY, SOUPY SALES, VIC LaVOLPE, DON and BEV PALMER, SAM PLUMERI, ROSE (SAM) DeWOLF, HARRY HARRIS, PAUL LEVINE, CLAIRE HUFF, WALT CANTER, STEVE FLANDERS, MAL WEST, MARK MONSKY, CIRO TORCHIA, KIRK NUROCK, CHUCK WIECHARD, ERIC COHEN, FRANK ZUBACK, BILL PETTIT, STEVE ("THE SCENE") PAUL, SANDY

OPPENHEIMER, BILL WINTERS and JACK (NIGHT TALK) McKINNEY. SY and MALVINA VOGEL, NATHAN A. FRIEDMAN, ESQ., MARV and MARSHA ROSENBERG, ARNIE SOMERS, STEVE SCHENKEL, FRED BERK, ALLEN DELIN, HARVEY and HARRIETT BLATT, LIPPY and SYLVIA EISNER, LEONARD G. FELDMAN, HARRIET HOROWITZ, SAM and BOOTSI COLODNY, MILTON LEVINE, BILL and LIL HOLSTEIN, MONIQUE VAUGEL, MARIO and MARGE PASCUCCI, NICK TOLKACH, ANN BOEKER, LEE J. MALTENFORT, LES ROBERTS, MIKE ROSENFELD and SUKEMASA YAGIHASHI and MICHIHIKO YAMATO, collegians.

SID SHLAK, LEON BROWN, JOE FRANKLIN, GODFREY (WEIGHT-WATCHER) CAMBRIDGE ED BROWN, JUDY EDELMAN, DEBBIE BAKER, CARMELA CANDELA, JACK CURTIS, JOEL DORN, LEN and NORA FISCHMAN, HARRY BOTOFF, BERNIE GOLDBERG, NEIL LEVENSON, DR. HOWARD LEVENSON, JULIUS (YUDEL) KAPLAN, IRWIN and HERBIE SPIEGEL, MARV HABAS, FRANK MARRERO, JIM TIGHE, DEBBIE MILLER, CHARLIE TRESKY, CHICK HALFON, FLORENCE FRIEDMAN, LENNIE WERKSTELL, FRAN SHANKIN, LILLIAN STUDNIA, WALT LAMOND, MARTIN and MIRIAM LAIBOW, KATHY MICHEL, LENNIE ORLAND, MEL (SHAKY) KUSHNER, METZ BERGER, ALVIN BERGER, SELMA FEGELSON, NORMAN LEIGHTON, BOB GOLDMAN, ARTHUR (TEN COPIES) AZARCHI, BUDDY (FLASH) MYERS, and JIM FRASCELLA of the A & P.

WILLIAM and DOLLY BANKS, JACK DASH, GEORGE WILSON, SID MARK, STEW CHASE, GEORGE LYLE, JIMMY CARTER, JOE HUNTER, BOB EVANS and RICK FRIEDMAN (all of WHAT-FM, Philadelphia), LOU DEITCH, NORMAN, PHYLLIS, MARK, DANA and JULIE SHAVIN.

CONG. CHARLES LONGSTREET WELTNER, DON TUCKER, BILL, MIKE and JEFF WILLIAMS, MR. and MRS. FORREST DUKE, LAURA TRACY, BOB JOYCE of KRAM, Vegas, DR. MICHAEL DEAN, COAST GUARD LT. COMDR. ED ARD, DR. and MRS. SEYMOUR LEDIS, BRUCE HUFF, MRS. DONALD L. RANSOM JR., PAMELA and GERALDINE LANDOU, PAUL S. HAYNIE, SID BRUMMEL, AL and THELMA BARON, CARL (KUSHELEH) ROSENTHAL, DAVID R. WEISMAN, PAUL DOBISH, RON LEVASSEUR, CHRISTIAN JACOBSEN, GEORGE COHEN, HUMPSIE and ABE FINKLE, MICKEY and HELEN DANER, GEORGE (JEEBEE) TEMKIN, LEW and EVELYN MARSHALL, KEN and CAROLE SYME, NORM and MARGE WEINSTEIN, LABRON SHUMAN (and his burnoose), and LINDA BILLINGTON.

JOE and CEIL BERKOWITZ, DR. RICHARD E. SELZNICK, LEN FEINBERG, LEON ROSENBERG, MEL (TWINKLE) STARR, IRWIN BODEE, WILLIE COHEN, MUFFY COHEN, HERBIE CLARK, NORM WISHNOW, JACK HAVESON, EUGENE HAVESON, LEN (FLOPPY) SWERDLOW, HERMAN KRAHN, HERB BRODY, JOE BELLITZ, MEYER BLOOM, JERRY HEYMAN, IRVING BUDDINE, RABBI WILLIAM FIERVERKER, ARLENE BERLIN, WALLACE WEINSTEIN, WARREN REDNOR, JERRY REDNOR, ABBIE BASH, IZZY POLLACK, RED NUSSBLATT, JOE ROGOFF, SHARKY ROSENTHAL, ACE AARONSON, TEDDY SNYDER, BARRY SNYDER, LON FRIEDMAN, GIL SUSSMAN, LOUISE STARK, ALAN HARRIS, BOB COWART, WILLIAM M. COWAN, MARC DROGIN, JEFFREY BYERLY, LEWIS LIPPIN, DR. EDWARD JAFFEE, RABBI BENJAMIN SINCOFF, CLEVELAND AMORY, ART ABRAMSOHN, JACK SHAW, and DAVE WISNIA.

ROBERT PINCUS, BILL and TURK TASHLIK, MAURICE POTOSKY, MRS. NELLIE GOETTEL, LARRY FUCHSBERG, CECE DANTZIG, MAX YOUNG, MARK, DIANA, SHIRA and MICHAEL GOLDMAN, BILL (VELVEL) SCHULMAN, BENNIE KEINER, SAMMY MORRIS, LARRY GELMAN, JACK and FRANCES ROSENBERG, JACK and SOPHIE ROSENBERG, DAVID NYMAN, DAVID VAN METER, CAROLE WOLFORD, SHYRLEE DALLARD, JOHN CARTER of A.G.A.C., VIC WOOLF, MRS. KIM MARSH, JOAN ALBERT of the Fontainebleau, PHIL ZELT, MO JAFFE and SGT. RICHARD LIPSHUTZ. PAUL GALLAGHER, EDDIE GOLDSTEIN, SAM BUSHMAN, HILDE SIMMONS, CONNIE KRATZOK, GWENDA TALENS, HAROLD (HESHY) STRAUSE, JOE and CHARLOTTE NASSAU, JERRY and MURIEL HIMMEL, JOSEPH McNAMARA, MAURY LEVY, MATT SLEEPER, MOISHE and BOOMIE SEGAL, IRV KERN, DR. LEONARD PHILLIPS, ARNOLD TOMOR, ISRAEL (COKE) RUBIN, DR. MILTON PALAT, DR. GEORGE ISAACSON, DR. ARNOLD KIMMEL, MARTIN and MINNA SAVAR, ABE and JERRY HERSH, ANDY FLAGER, BUS SAIDT, YALE RABINOWITZ, SAUL ROSSIEN, MILTON FEINBERG, PHIL (FIFEL) BLOOM, NATE, SAM and FRED MELMAN, TEDDY FLAER, PHIL MILLSTEIN, IRV DANA, NORMAN STERN, HARVEY STERN, SHIRLEY MERRIMAN, and NICK MEGLIN.

JACK (ELEPHANT BOY) WALSH, BARRY REISMAN, MELVIN KARTZMER, LEON KARTZMER, CHARLIE PAPIER, DONNIE PAPIER, BARBARA SYKES, MOLLY LEVINE, JOE CANNON, HAZEL SWEENEY, ROGER GLACKIN, CLAIRE MILLER, MR. and MRS. GERRY FINN, BENNIE MOSKOWITZ and JULES RESNICK.

MRS. HELEN MEYNER, HAROLD MAY, BOB BURTON, JIM POWERS, JACK HELSEL, J. WELLINGTON PIDCOCK, HORACE GREELEY McNAB, COUSIN DAVE GOMBERG, DAVE (OLDTIMER) HORWITZ, RON SCOTT, CHRIS WINNER, GABE ROSEN, CARL (KIVVY) ABROMOVITZ, DR. LEWIS HIRSH, SCOTTY MOSOVICH, MAYNARD BARKER, BOB AMOROS, SAM (TAMMI) KAPLAN, JACKIE and ARNOLD HODES, DAVE PITASKY, DAVE, WILLIE and MENDY KRAVITZ, JOE BERGER, JERRY, SIDNEY, MARTY, RALPH, ALFRED and IVAN POPKIN, IRV WARACH, ELI WARACH, ROBERT OLINSKY, BENNY OLINSKY, LOUIE OLINSKY, MILTON OLINSKY, IRV OLIN, CHARLIE BYER, RABBI WILLIAM, NATIE, JERRY and SIDNEY GORDON, JACKIE and WALTER HARRISON, WALT BELLAK, JACK POLLACK, PAT POLLACK, PAUL CAGAN, HARVEY SILK, MARK LITOWITZ, HARRY ZOLTICK, ALLAN and WALLY PLAPINGER, ERWIN WAINER, HYMAN (COWBOY) BALITZ, SHELDON SEAVEY, ZIGGY WALDMAN, CLYDE LEIB, EMIL SLABODA, HARVEY YAVENER, JOE LOGUE, EDDIE GOLDEN, ED (DUFFY) RAMSEY, EDDIE SOLAN, STEVE MERVISH and GEORGE MOLDOVAN. MURRAY BURNETT, BOB MENEFEE, TED REINHART, MIKE McGRADY, ABEL GREEN, NORMA NANNINI, BILL KARDALEY, ANDY ETTINGER, NATE ROBERTS, NORM BROOKS, ELAINE BELK, DURWARD EARLY, BERT and MIKE WEILAND, MARK VAN BROOKS, TOMMY THOMPSON, BETTY STEVENS, JAY (FINE SWISS WATCHES) GOLD, SYLVIA MANDELL, B. A. BERGMAN, FRANK BROOKHOUSER, WAYNE and AGNES ROBINSON, DAVID and STEVE KUSHELOFF, MURRAY, MARILYN, DEBBY and HOLLY ARNOLD, FREDERICK WERTHEIMER, AL FINGERMAN, HY and MARILYN GARDNER, FLORENCE BLOCK, DAVE WEST, CHARLIE SCOTT, EARL JOSEPHSON, MURRAY FISHER, JULI BAINBRIDGE, SHELDON WAX, ED, ROSE, WENDY and STEVEN BURTON, BOBBY DARIN, DON BARBER, TEDDI LEVISON, MICKIE SILVERSTEIN, RALPH COLLIER, BILL STRETCH, STEVE O'KEEFE, COL. CHARLES GREGG, CHARLIE PETZOLD, DON SCOTT, RUTH OLIS, FRANK MULLOY, HILDA SHIVERS, BOB RITCHIE, HOWARD MacDOUGALL, RALPH PEARL, JOE STEAD, FRANK WATRING, BOB (BOOKSTORES) CRAIG, BILL LINK and DICK LEVINSON, and SID and BUNNY SHORE.

MERV GRIFFIN and TONY GAROFALO, RUBE VERIN, BEN GRAFF, CHARLIE HERB and AL AMBERG of RUBE'S BARBER SHOP, Levittown, Pa., FRANK BISANZIO, LOU EMANUEL, EARL GEORGE of A.F.T.R.A., RON POLAO, LOU SCHEINFELD and JAY SARNO, JIMMIE (THE GREEK) SNYDER, RON AMOS, NATHAN JACOBSON, DAVID VICTORSON and MAURY, MURIEL and BRUCE STEVENS of Caesar's Palace, Vegas. JOHN HUEGHNERGARTH, artist, MR. and MRS. JERRY GAGHAN, SID SHUCKER, GEORGE BLAISDELL, JACK McCUTCHEON, LEWIS CHARLES WENDELL JR., JERRY VERBEL, WILLIAM B. WILLIAMS, FLORENCE LONDONER, DR. JULES K. LEVY, JERRY SCHLOSS, ROBERT (LAUGHTRACK) PEET, BERNARD ZELL, MICHAEL SPOLL, APRIL AARONS, ISADORE SOLOVAY, MARTY MOSKOWITZ, JANE SCHULZE, CY and CLAIRE NEIBURG, JACK and BARBARA GILL, BARBARA KELLMAN, DON PHILLIPS, TOM (CONTACT, KYW-TV, Philly) SNYDER, DONALD E. KNOX, STAN BERK, DIANE ACTMAN, JIM TATE, and DR. WALDO FIELDING, ART MOGER, GEORGE ESTES, AL SHERMAN, MILT YAKUS, MIKE REINGOLD, GEORGE ROBERTS, DAVID HOFF, IRA GOLDBLATT, RICHARD C. JACOBS, AL KORN, JESS CAIN and LENNY MEYERS of the TUB THUMPERS, Boston.

And... NANCY BROWN LEVINE of Plainfield, NJ.-Poughkeepsie, N.Y.

Table of Contents

PROLOGUE

We have an old saying in the Israeli Secret Service well worth committing to memory, Mr. Bond. Briefly, it is this:

If you meet a man for the first time and he discharges a pistol in your direction it could be he's a nervous, insecure person hungering for some attention or even sympathy in this increasingly dehumanized world.

If on your second meeting he makes a threatening gesture with a machete it could be a manifestation of a severe sexual aberration since, as we now know from Hollywood films, a knife is a penile symbol.

But should you meet the same man a third time and he attempts to take your life by using curare, cyanide, low-yield nuclear weapon or one of those extra-fat-drenched hamburgers sold by a firm whose name will not be mentioned here, and cries out, "Die, Israeli dog!" then such behavior can only be construed as out and out bellicosity, justifying at the very least a nasty letter to the New York Times (no more than 500 words please), or even a physical response of some sort.

- M

1

Mondo Bondo

Two hours to Tokyo, where he would rendezvous with Baron Cockimamiyama Sanka, the *ichi-ban*[*] of the *Kyodo Kikaku*,[**] Israel Bond was jolted out of a demon-haunted nap by a rapid-fire sequence of sounds:

> ... The snatch of song in a lilting, ingenuous Irish brogue:
> "Ivory liquid helps yer hands feel young again..."
> ... A horrified shriek.
> ... A metallic thump against the left wing of the Japan Air Lines superjet.

Gottenu! The realization of what had occurred cast him into utter despair.

We've collided with Mary Mild.

He awoke in a chilling sweat to find upon him the solicitous eyes of the enchanting kimonoed and obied stewardess, the maiden called Festering Wind.

"It was bound to happen sooner or later, Mr. Bond. Miss Mild's frequent, haphazard flights as a soap company's television spokeswoman through congested air corridors have endangered hundreds of commercial planes. However"—and her manner was reassuring—"it was just a glancing blow. I am confident of her ability to make it to Guam or Wake for any necessary repairs to her body or starched apron."

Quite the charmer, this Festering Wind, Bond thought; *something more than the typical, efficient JAL servant of the sky dispensing*

---

[*]   Number one
[**]   Japanese Secret Service

her ever-handy supply of fluffy pillows and bowls of green tea. For
Festering Wind was also one of Baron Sanka's most trusted
agents and under orders to accord Bond the super-deluxe
treatment a guest of his stature warranted. When the Baron
called for VIP service he did not stint. The jet's first-class
compartment, customarily catering to sixteen people, had been
revamped for Bond's sole use and closed off from the tourist
section by a bamboo curtain. Its seats had been ripped out
to make space for a contoured swivel-chair bed under which
thrummed a Relaxacizor unit; an *ofuro*, the deep, tiled Japanese
bath now abubble with lethal chunks of Blofeld blowfish; a well-
stocked bar with such offbeat libations as Creme de Mousse (the
tiny antlers had been removed); a massage table; and a stereo
corner which had already regaled him with *Senator Dirksen and
Congressman Powell Recite the All-Time Top Forty Hymns* and at
present was pumping out a catchy medley, "You're the Top,"
"You Can Do Anything Better than We Can" and "What Can We
Say, Sir, After We Say We're Sorry?" all from the new LP *The
Beatles Apologize to Jesus at the Astrodome.*

In her frequent capacity as a masseuse Festering Wind had
become accustomed and therefore indifferent to the bodies of
magnificent men—sumo wrestlers, karate masters, *kendo* stick
experts and the like—yet she shivered whenever her fingers
strayed over the musculature of this *gaijin*[*] clad only in an extra-
long, extra-wide Carnaby Street Mod tie (all he actually needed
in the way of clothing, so generous was the amount of the tie's
material). But aroused as she was by the massive shoulders, a
trim waist that was more Hebraic than wasp, and long, tapering
fingers, she found herself transfixed again and again by the
cruel, darkly handsome face marked by a whitish scar on the left
cheek (or was it the right? It seemed to be constantly *shifting!)*
and the sorrow misting the gray eyes. Surely, she deduced, this
man has suffered a monumental loss in his recent past.

Bond extracted a filter-tipped Raleigh from a pack Scotch-
taped to his left thigh and ignited a blue-tipped Ohio match
with a rub inside an abrasive furrow of skin perched atop his
right shoulder, a memento of a madman's Luger bullet in the
unbelievable Loxfinger business of 1965. "How long was I in
dreamy Dreamsville, my pet?"

"You shuttered those haunted eyes an hour before we
landed in Hawaii to refuel, Mr. Bond. I had not the heart to wake

---

[*]   Foreigner

you. And Baron Sanka's orders were explicit. I am to let you rest whenever possible."

"Man, that Sanka really lets you sleep," Bond marveled.

On chopsticks whittled from the softest balsa wood that grows in the gardens of the Meiji Shrine, she fed him *hershi-sushi*, those succulent squares of chocolate-covered squid so highly prized by Japan's upper class. Then it was time for his hourly massage, and to make up for the ones he'd missed while asleep, Festering Wind decided to put something special into it—herself. Peeling off his Mod tie and her diaphanous kimono and utilizing every wile taught to her by Madam Making-the-Bird-Rise of the Nishi Academy of Sexual Stimulation and Fish Cleaning, she led him through the flowery gateway of her being, their stamens and pistils dissolving in the searing instant of their cross-pollination. *Gottenu!* he sobbed soundlessly. *I never dreamed it could be this way again. She's got my mojo* * *working and I love it! Oh, Sarah, Sarah, my lost angel. Forgive me again for my callous infidelity.*

An astral shape materialized over his head; two reproachful black eyes peered over a veil into his guilty, flinching gray ones. *I forgive you, Iz, my darling. But don't enjoy it too much.*

I won't, I won't, his heart pledged.

But somehow he did.

After it was done and she'd swept away the last soggy petal the ecstatic Festering Wind glided to a rack and wheeled over a load of books and newspapers. "I picked these up in Honolulu, sir. Would you care to read?"

His ebullience flown, Bond stared at his moody reflection in the Perspex and gave a listless shrug. He jammed one of the new super-length Benson & Hedges into his sensual mouth, maneuvered the tip so that it would touch a flickering candle on the bar two feet away and inhaled deeply, blowing out fifty-four smoke rings, twenty-three octagons and the word "antidisestablishmentarianism." He thumbed through the books—*The Wit and Wisdom of Lester Maddox, God's Answers to Children's Letters, No, You Can't!* (a new biography of Sammy Davis by a Mississippi sheriff) and *Frodo's Hobbit Cookbook*, discarding them as too depressing. His heart quickened momentarily as he saw under the pile the Sunday *New York Times*, of all the world's newspapers his absolute favorite. (Bond had long considered himself the perfect amalgam of brains and brawn—erudite

---

*   Male member (Shikoku dialect)

enough to understand the Sunday *New York Times*; strong enough
to carry it.) But the advertisements in the slick magazine section,
so captivating as a rule, left him oddly unmoved—the dewy-eyed
sylph in scanties and a judicial wig: "I dreamed I refuted the
findings of the Warren Commission in my Maidenform Bra";
the dour spokesman in the rent-a-car pitch: "We'd love to make
Number Two all over Number One."

Nor was there the slightest appeal in the cavalcade of
inanities that constituted the front-page stories. An extremist
civil rights group had made vociferous demands for "Black
Power!"—at the main office of General Electric. The spirit of
ecumenism continued to proliferate; a Vatican emissary gifted
a prominent Jewish organization with a replica of the famous
Papal encyclical on "Peace on Earth," *Pacem in Terris*; the latter
had reciprocated by mailing the Holy See the ancient Hassidic
treatise on child psychology, *Pacem in Tuchas*. In New Haven, a
campus "mating" computer, fed data on key socioeconomic and
sexual factors, had concluded that the ideal marital partner
for a Yale man was another Yale man. America's urban riots
would be the theme of a new Broadway musical, *Sniper on the
Roof*. United Press International columnist Dick West had
interviewed a Monterey, California, youth arrested for stabbing
nineteen policemen and setting afire ten houses of worship.
"My incarceration is illegal and an affront to creative people
everywhere," the youth lamented. "What hope is there for the
artist if the authorities cannot comprehend the improvisational
nature of a 'happening'?"

Bond tossed the *Times* aside for the *Pacific Stars & Stripes*,
the sprightly tabloid that services America's fighting men
throughout the Far East.

And the bold-faced lead story lashed out at him like the
tongue of a cobra.

Carrying the byline of columnist Al Ricketts, the story was
datelined Kagoshima, Japan.

A Lieutenant Eno Nanonuni, commander of an Imperial
Japanese patrol boat, had reported contacting an unidentified
fishing trawler "violating our territorial waters. I deployed our
craft so close to the intruder that I could clearly see the glazed,
mad-dog eyes of the crew, who were hanging over the rail and
spouting epithets of a particularly offensive nature, relating
as they did to our beloved Emperor. I also saw nets laden with
illegally harvested fish."

Ordered to halt and receive a boarding party, the trawler responded by raking the patrol boat with machine-gun fire, wounding Lieutenant Nanonuni and three of his men. "I replied in kind," the officer stated, "by ordering a brace of torpedoes to be put into her below the waterline. She sank at once. There were no survivors. I sent down a diver, who identified the drowned men as Caucasians and emerged with two souvenirs, the log and flag. The former indicated the vessel was the *Blintz Charming,* of Haifa registry, commanded by Captain Jacob Bar-Kochlefel, and the route of passage the Suez Canal, Indian Ocean, Strait of Malacca, South China Sea and a final entry, Kagoshima. The latter was even more intriguing. It bears the Star of David."

The *Pacific Stars & Stripes* fluttered from Bond's agitated hands to the floor. "The Bernardi," he whispered out of his suddenly taut throat. "Hand me the Bernardi."

Sensing the alarm in his request, Festering Wind flashed an enticing length of leg as she reached up to the overhead rack, unlocked the instrument case and gently deposited in his lap the violin carved out of huge blocks of vermicelli by the sixteenth-century Jew, Erschelli Bernardi, in the opinion of many the superior of Da Vinci in cartography, painting, alchemy (Bernardi had transformed gold into peat moss) and sophisticated weaponry. The second he tucked it under his sensual dewlaps he felt the cordovan-stained pasta radiating a mystical glow throughout his body. On the upper right side of the violin was the raised, two-inch copper Seal Of Bernardi, its somewhat vulgar acronym glinting in the first rays of the Eastern sun. For those of limited intellect a Stradivarius or an Amati would be quite adequate, thank you, but the minuscule handful of true stringed-instrument aficionados would settle for nothing less than a "Bernie." Alas, the floods that had ravaged Florence had buried all of the Old World's Bernardis in the muck and in all of creation there were but three extant, one owned by Heifetz, another by Henny Youngman and the third cradled in the reverent arms of Israel Bond, now en route to "the calm beauty of Japan at slightly under the speed of sound."[*]

When inexplicable events dictated a session of cogitation, Bond often found scraping the yellowed but still supple iguana-gut strings an invaluable aid in cranking up his mental processes. The gray eyes narrowed; the muscles of the right arm coaxed a spirited series of *cadenzas* and *wallendas* from the third move-

---

[*]   Courtesy of the Japan Air Lines brochure.

ment of the *Emilio Largo* and he leaned back to mull over the shocking item from the *Pacific Stars & Stripes.*

Gottenu! So that was the gruesome fate of the *Blintz Charming!* It had been a mystery bedeviling the Israeli Ministry of Fisheries, who in desperation had thrown it to M 33 and the Secret Service. The trawler had been missing for weeks. No last-second SOS had ever been transmitted; no debris spotted on the Mediterranean. Now it had turned up in Japan, "The Land of the Rising Datsun," to perpetrate a senseless attack on an Imperial craft. What the hell was going on here? Soon he'd be beseeching Baron Sanka for a helping hand in tracking down Dr. Ernst Holzknicht, sole survivor of the Nazi murder gang, the Terrorist Union for Suppressing Hebrews, TUSH,[*] that Bond had wrecked in the Queen caper—Holzknicht, the diabolical genius whose "Operation Alienation" had come within a whisker of wiping out Judaism; Holzknicht, who'd metamorphosed a joyous June wedding day into horror by murdering under the canopy Bond's wife-to-be, the mysterious veiled rider of the desert, Sarah Lawrence of Arabia. And how disposed would Sanka be to lending that hand after this slap in the face from Bond's adopted homeland?

He sawed away at the Bernardi for a few minutes, coming up with an acceptable ending to Schubert's "Unfinished" Symphony—the seven notes that signified "Shave and a haircut, two bits!"— and wondered why the composer hadn't resolved his problem that simply. Good-o! His mind was clicking on both cylinders. Now he had to rid his body of its sloth. To accomplish this he handed the Bernardi to the girl, opened the bamboo curtain and commenced a punishing chain of traveling pushups, deep elbow-and-knee bends and cartwheels down the aisle of the tourist section, which would not only start the vital juices coursing again but also allow him to check out any new arrivals on at Honolulu, a solid bit of security technique always to be practiced by an agent carrying an Oy Oy license to kill.

The passengers, all familiar to him since he'd boarded in San Francisco, were dozing. Except the new one in Seat 26A.

Crooning a prayer, "O mani pod may hom,"[**] his fork-bearded chin dug into a pot of a belly, was a moon-faced Oriental in the saffron robe of a monk. His sagacious black eyes scanned Bond's intent expression and twinkled fractionally.

[*]   Which rhymes with "push," and that means there's trouble, big
      trouble, in River City.
[**] Hail to the jewel in Tiffany's window!

"My son." The voice was low-keyed, irresistible. "There is a great sadness in your face. Sit by me and let me attempt to bring a little solace into your life. You have lost someone dear to you, is it not so?"

Bond, a grim smile on his sensual lips, slid in beside the newcomer. This was either a holy man blessed with acute perception or... someone in "the game."

"You seem to know much about me, holy one."

"It is my training, my son. I am the monk Aw Gee Minh, so named because my mother gave birth to me in a Hong Kong theater featuring an old Wallace Beery film. I am returning to my strife-torn land of Vietnam following a tour of Hawaii on a Rambler Foundation grant."

"Rambler?"

"I applied too late to procure one from Ford. In Honolulu I was privileged to attend the Congress of Revelations by Acknowledged Psychics, the highlight of which was the candlelight wedding of Edgar Cayce to Bridey Murphy. We toasted the happy couple with glasses of Reincarnation Milk. Now let us consider your condition. Life's vicissitudes have hurt you deeply. To revitalize your life force and start you on the road to *satori* or enlightenment, we must conduct a *mondo*, which is a Zen Buddhist dialogue between a monk and an acolyte. The dialogue may seem trivial, but it is a valid tool for probing the innermost secrets of the heart. Before we begin it will be necessary to purify our mouths of any hateful words lingering from past conversations." He produced a paper packet from somewhere in the robe's folds, slit it open with a deft thumbnail and poured some black specks into his palm and Bond's. "Let us eat them, my son. They will produce phrases of sweetness and grace."

Bond wolfed down the dots. "How spicy they are, holy one. What are they called?"

"Zen-Zen. Now the *mondo*. I shall put to you questions of an abstract nature and you will respond to the best of your ability. Question One: *What will you do if they ask you to kill the cuckoo?*"

"I shall stand in front of the clock and shield it with my body, if need be."

"Excellent! Despite your grief, you continue to display compassion. Second: *What will you do if they force you to kill the cuckoo?*"

"I shall kill them. But who *are* they?"

"Why do you ask?"

"I must know. I have a right to know. I have a feeling the cuckoo wants to know."

"Why should the cuckoo want to know? It is only a bird."

"Hath not a bird the right to know? Hath it not eyes, ears, nose and throat? If ye prick it, will it not bleed?"

They were moving ever closer to the arcane meaning of the *mondo*, the monk making cuckoo-like noises, Bond doing his obscure and difficult impression of John Byner imitating Kirk Douglas imitating Frank Gorshin, when the girl's urgent cry halted it. "Mr. Bond, please return to your compartment."

Bond, a trifle miffed, rose reluctantly. "Forgive me, holy one. My governess calls. I can't thank you enough for your concern. I've learned much about life in these simple exchanges. At least I now know that life is not a fountain."

"If it is anything, life is the Fontainebleau in Miami Beach, my son," Aw Gee Minh said sententiously. "Farewell. We shall meet again in the place where there is no darkness."

"And no cuckoo," Bond said with touching tenderness.

Back in his quarters, Bond told Festering Wind, "The interruption was quite unnecessary. He was a harmless, well-meaning old coot trying to do me some good in his own way."

"I am sorry, Mr. Bond, but the Baron also ordered me to keep close surveillance on you. A man in your profession faces constant peril. And besides, it is time for your next MacLuhan massage."

She once more removed his Mod tie and he vaulted onto the table. Her hands, of surprising strength for one so slight, were assiduous octopi on his ankles, calves and buttocks and he felt the chronic soreness fleeing these spots to settle permanently in his neck and shoulder muscles.

Suddenly he sensed tension in her hands and speech.

"All good things come in threes. Said Peter Gunn: 'You'd better muzzle that badly trained mutt who's on top of us.'"

He caught it at once, the cipher she was formulating after the key word "threes." *Gunn... muzzle... trained... on... us.*

The derisive voice said, "And what will you do, Oy Oy Seven, if the cuckoo turns on you and bites you in the TUSH?"

The silencer coughed twice and he heard Festering Wind's "Oh" and felt her hands slide off his thighs. She crumpled at the foot of the massage table, a widening stain on her breast.

Fanatical eyes aglitter, the monk pushed through the curtain. "I also understand a simple three-cipher, Mr. Bond."

Smoke wafted up from the silencer attachment on the Toppo-Gigio, the little Italian mini-Mauser.

"You needn't have killed the girl."

"A maiden who knows ciphers and has strong hands is far too dangerous to let live, my son."

"So the good, wise monk is a TUSH-y?"[*]

"Ah, my *mondo* was not in vain. You have indeed grasped the meaning of life. Now my Toppo-Gigio will impart the meaning of death."

"Who are you?"

"An old enemy, Mr. Bond. I had boarded this aircraft with a purpose. To destroy it. Imagine my glee at discovering your presence and realizing I could accomplish my primary mission and even two old scores to the bargain." The gun wielder emitted a hard, cough-like laugh that sounded like his silencer. "Part of what I told you, Oy Oy Seven, is true. I am Aw Gee Minh from Vietnam but it should not take you an eternity to conclude what half of that nation claims my allegiance. I am the younger brother of that master of Communist guerrilla warfare Vi Teh Minh, whom you destroyed on the cigar-shaped Caribbean isle of El Tiparillo.[**] Long has his spirit cried out for vengeance."

"And the second score?" Bond's query was nonchalant as his right hand inched toward his mezuzah, the cylindrical symbol of his faith dangling on a chain around his neck.

"I'm afraid that won't do at all, Mr. Bond," the monk said equably, but the mouth twisted into a sneer, the fat forefinger squeezed the Toppo-Gigio's trigger twice and it splashed its molten message into Bond's body, the first severing the chain and nicking his neck, the second hammering into his right shoulder. Bond, battered to his knees by the one-two punch, gazed in disbelief at the bloodburst from the gouged-out shoulder top. Slug Two had whistled through the furrow of skin, flattening both sides. Through the haze of pain he thought, *Well, there goes the best damn match-scratcher a man ever had. But what's he waiting for? I'm exsanguinating like a butchered steer. Where's the finisher through the heart or between my sensual gray eyes?*

"By now, Oy Oy Seven, your modus operandi is well known to us. That mezuzah and its hidden dart tipped with Molochamovis-B venom is far safer on the floor, don't you agree? To continue: The second score I shall repay involves a niece who

---

[*]　An agent of TUSH
[**]　*Matzohball*, 1966, $1.00.

once was one of our topnotch agents until she was subverted by
your sexuality in the so-called Loxfinger affair. You will recall
Nu Kee, whose cover role was that of 'Miss Vietcong' in the
beauty pageant."

"Yes," Bond panted. "A fine girl corrupted by your
expansionist doctrines until I inserted a large"—he paused,
seeking a tactful phrase—"Hebrew point of view. What has
befallen her?"

"She died by my hand after we caught her working for the
Americans in Saigon. Familial feelings have no place in this
business."

The blood kept gurgling from Bond's shoulder and he bit his
lip to fight off the tides of darkness threatening to sweep him
into unconsciousness. "This primary mission you alluded to..."

"In a few minutes," Aw Gee Minh said in a pedagogical
manner, "after your demise, of course, I shall stroll into the
pilots' deck, place my weapon against the captain's neck and
command him to radio Haneda Airport that his plane is being
hijacked by a crazed member of the Shinbet.* After he has
made contact I shall shoot him and the copilot, set the plane on
automatic control to keep it airborne awhile longer and step out
of the door. My minichute will unfurl and during my descent to
the Pacific I shall fire a Veery pistol so that the hydrofoil waiting
for me at a certain coordinate will spot the flare and take me
from the life raft presently tucked about my midsection. A
hundred or more passengers from many nations will perish and
Israel will be blamed for an insensate act, as the good *Herr Doktor*
planned. Japan, in particular, will be outraged."

"Holzknicht again." The despairing words rasped out of
Bond's bone-dry throat. "How were you recruited into this
cabal?"

"Dr. Holzknicht has quite a file on those holding grudges
against Israel and, more specifically, against you, Oy Oy Seven.
Now the *mondo* ends. The cuckoo calls."

"Wait! I beg of you, wait!"

"How disappointing," the monk smirked. "The celebrated
Israel Bond begs for his life like some common cutpurse."

"Not for myself, holy one. For humanity. Take the Bernardi
with you when you jump."

---

* Sherutei Betahan, an early version of an Israeli intelligence force.
  Len Deighton's books contain loads of "inside" references like
  this. They also have skillful plots and meaty characterizations...
  if that's what you want... S.W.

The monk's brows knitted in puzzlement. "But this is extraordinary. The glorious strains filtering back to the tourist section were not recorded? You possess a genuine Bernardi?"

"On my seat. See for yourself."

A circumspect left eye followed Bond's forefinger. "It is true. Capital! It will bring no less than twenty million colodnys into the coffers of TUSH when I peddle it in Macao. Your chance remark, Mr. Bond, has earned you another five minutes of life."

"Shoot and get it over with."

"No, my friend. Pick it up and play for me."

Bond drew himself up with as much dignity as his bloodied frame would permit. He grunted a coarse biological suggestion to his adversary.

The monk chuckled. "For your information, Mr. Bond, I happen to be a pure hermaphrodite who can do and have done countless times precisely what you suggest. But you have forgotten one of the cardinal precepts of a membership in TUSH. A foe is not only to be vanquished but, when possible, humiliated to the nth degree. Pick up the Bernardi, Secret Agent Oy Oy Seven."

"I refuse. Do your worst."

He saw the slow rise of the Toppo-Gigio and whispered the *Sh'ma Israel*. It coughed; there was a buzz-saw sound and he paled as the copper Seal Of Bernardi flew off the violin into the seething *ofuro*.

"You bastard! You've desecrated a masterpiece."

"Not at all, Mr. Bond. My perfect shot merely drove the seal off its hinges. However, my next shots will crunch the violin into splinters unless you serenade me with no further delay. Pick it up. Good. Now, in this order I want you play and sing 'The Horst Wessel Song,' 'The Internationale' and finally the number-one song on the Southeast Asian Hit Parade, 'The Thoughts of Chairman Mao.'"

Bond positioned the Barnardi against his claret-soaked shoulder. The swine! His captor had chosen three songs calculated to turn the stomach of any Jew: the Brown Shirt hymn and its boast of impaling Jews on knives; the old Communist anthem, mocking him with its reminder of more than three million of his kin entrapped by the Jew-baiting Soviet regime; and the sycophantic paean to the xenophobic old Leninist who threatened to send the hordes of Han rolling over the world.

No matter. If by sating the TUSH-y's lust for degradation he could preserve a priceless Jewish artifact, then his personal debasement was inconsequential. He launched into the first "request" in guttural Berliner German, letting his defeated gray eyes absorb die indescribable loveliness of the Bernardi for the last time. Where the seal had been were four tiny holes, each housing one of the hinges, and he felt a profound relief. A competent metalsmith could heat the Seal Of Bernardi, pound it back into shape and insert it into the pasta with little or no visible damage. And, of course, the monk, after he'd put the quietus on Bond, would fish into the *ofuro* to retrieve it. He'd have to, to guarantee the instrument's authenticity.

Midway through "The Internationale" his body began to shake and he heard the monk snicker: "Fear pervades the invincible Oy Oy Seven?" but he ignored it. He allowed a sickly grin to crease his lips and carefully lowered his eyes to the section of the violin laid bare by the removal of the seal. A definite message carved in elegant curlicues! But in what language? Italian? Latin? No! By thunder, Yiddish!

He was playing and singing about "the final conflict," his heart thumping intricate paradiddles Max Roach or Buddy Rich never could have duplicated, while he screamed at his brain: *Translate! Translate!*

Now he was on the whining Cantonese song, one cylinder of his brain concentrating on the decipherment of the tortuous Yiddish paragraph.

> I met you in a commune
> Under a Peking moon,
> Thanks to the thought of Chairman Mao!

> *Mine bridder* Yid—*my brother Jew—if at this moment you are held at bay by an anti-Semite...*

> The poster on the wall
> Said in love we'd fall,
> Thanks to the thought of Chairman Mao!

> *... button on the bow...*

> We filled up jars of night soil,
> A task we found divine;

I filled mine with your night soil,
You stuffed your jar with mine!

*... exposes a notch into which you may insert the
iguana-gut string closest to your right hand, the
pressure from which...*

We sauntered through the town,
And painted the town brown,
And heard a "well done" cheer from Lin Paio!

*... releases from the tip of the bow a steel shaft dipped
in a compost of ingredients...*

There was gladness in the eye
Of good old Chou En-lai,
And we knew we'd hurt revisionism—and how!
Thanks to the thought,
The blinding thought,
the thought of Chairman...
A good man and a fair man,
The thought ... of ... Chairman Maaaaaaaaoooo...
oh voh dee o doh!

"In truth, Mr. Bond, I have never heard it sung so well,
not even by the Red Guard Tabernacle Choir. You missed your
calling, my friend. Had you chosen the profession of a music hall
minstrel you would have enjoyed a long, venerable life. Goodbye,
Secret Agent Oy Oy Seven."

The pudgy gun hand pointed the Toppio-Gigio straight at
the heart of Israel Bond.

But the drawn iguana-gut string had twanged its Nashville
Sound, propelling the bow-turned-arrow from the violin-turned-
bow. Deep into the right cheek of Aw Gee Minh burrowed the
discolored tip of the steel shaft. The bow swayed back and forth,
a maddened pendulum of death. In creepy fascination Bond
saw the moon face change from yellow to a revolting purple
as the still lethal venom on the shaft tip—a mixture of bizarre
elements like belladarvi, hemlock paste and warlock droppings
found only in that infamous region of Italy known as the Borgia
Belt—diffused through the capillaries.

Aw Gee Minh's body was a Macy's Thanksgiving Day parade balloon suddenly deflated. The knees turned to rubber, caved in and he fell ponderously on his moon face.

"The poison was in the violin," jibed Bond. "Isn't that enough to drive you... cuckoo?"

The black vortex had him helpless in its grasp now and he surrendered to the inexorable tides. As he slumped against the massage table his last recollections were of his Jewish brother who'd sent him a message of salvation across the centuries; his feeble jest, "Saved by an SOB!" and the popeyed Japan Air Lines purser charging into the compartment....

During a blessed spell of unconsciousness Israel Bond found time to reflect upon the decision that was sending him winging to the exotic Far Eastern land where, the cognoscenti will tell you, the cherry blossoms best around the age of fourteen.

2
The Historical Verity

A month before, Israel Bond, at the wheel of a 1967 Nader, the world's safest sports car (it was constructed of panels of Campfire marshmallows, which upon impact would fluff up into spongy billows to cushion the driver), turned off the Strip into the driveway of Fabulous Las Vegas' newest, gaudiest address, Caesars Palace, that twenty-five-million-dollar Roman orgy with crap tables. He guided the Nader under each of the thirteen spewing fountains to gain a free car wash, then squealed to a halt at the entrance, where two collections of statuary quickly established the resort's classical motif: *The Rape of the Sabine Women* and *The Sabine Women Seen Consulting with Alan Dershowitz and Melvin Belli.*

"*Salve!*" chirped a bellhop in a centurion's uniform, who proceeded to unload Bond's Ventura-Condoli luggage.

"*Lesbia est puella,*" Bond countered, drawing upon his storehouse of Catullan maxims.

"Well, that's *de rerum natura,* I guess," the bellhop conceded and ushered Bond to Caesars Palace's preferred suite for big spenders, the Maximus Rabinowus. Waiting within, as the coded cable from Jerusalem had told him she would be, was M.'s new secretary, Lobsang Rampapport, a Tibetan who'd made a recent conversion to Judaism, her luscious, lipogenic limbs revealed by a spangled Vestal Virgin minitoga.

"We shall beat our spears into pruning hooks," the girl said self-consciously, pausing to allow Bond to complete the countersign.

"And our prunes into compote," Bond retorted. He made the bellhop's eyes bulge with a crisp two-hundred-salazar tip and two center-aisle tickets to *Cabaret* and shooed him out. "So you're M.'s new right arm? And you're all excited about this espionage crap, the passwords and such. Kid, get out of this lousy racket before you end up like Lilah Tov." His voice cracked on the adored name of the beauteous brunette who'd died so horribly in the Queen caper.

Lobsang's mouth tightened and he knew his warning had sunk in. Two of her eyes remained steadfast and clear, but her third eye wept copiously in memory of her predecessor.

In the days that followed, a legend was born along the Vegas Strip about a dark, cruelly handsome man whose grey eyes sought something on the horizon beyond the ken of mortal men... a man ferried from casino to casino in a Caesars Palace VIP golden chariot pulled by six haughty Arabian steeds and driven by a dashing charioteer named Ben Hur-Owitz... a man whose wanton gambling reduced the high-stakes exploits of Nick the Greek to Little League size.

Israel Bond... Israel Bond... Israel Bond...

His name was whispered at the Desert Inn, where he smashed the bank at *la guerre;*[*] by the dealer at the Flamingo, who quailed at Bond's icy calm: "You've just picked the Old Maid from my hand, old chap. You're done..." which meant a loss to the house of seventy-eight million dollars; and at the Thunderbird, where he fired a sizzling twelve-under-par 62 on the miniature golf course to humble the resident pro, Slammin' Sammy Schneid, who boggled at Bond's incredible curling birdie putt through the treacherous maze of Pepsi-Cola cans on the sixteenth green.

On a fateful Sunday night at Caesars Palace, fourteen distinguished men in Savile Row suitings of Phil Harris tweed clustered outside Bond's suite. They were the distraught owners of the Strip's major hotels and they'd been stung for a collective loss of seven hundred million dollars.

"Gentlemen." Mr. Tropicana opened the discussion. "This Bond guy has racked us up but good. What's to be done about it?"

"Nothing," said Mr. Sands. "I had my spotters watching Bond on the hidden TV over the Old Maid table. The son of a bitch plays like a maniac, like there's no tomorrow, but he's

---

[*]   The world's most sophisticated card game. See *On The Secret Service of His Majesty, the Queen*, the third Israel Bond thriller. Its title earned me the commendation of "Honorary Homosexual."—S.W.

honest. Funny thing... every so often he looks off into space and mumbles, 'Sarah, Sarah!' over and over."

"Wonder where he got his original jackroll?" asked Mr. Aladdin. "He couldn't have run up seven hundred mil that fast without big front money. And I hear through the grapevine that he's even rejected an invitation to dine with Howard Hughes."

"I can answer that," put in Mr. Caesars Palace, inhaling his White Owl. "Before he came to Caesars Palace he'd made a killing on the market. When the Tall Texan at 1600 Pennsylvania Avenue gave a certain type of dessert his enthusiastic Good Whitehousekeeping Seal of Approval at a widely covered press conference, Bond, who'd been tipped that the endorsement was coming, moved fast, got his people at the Dreyfus Fund to corner fifty thousand shares of Minute Tapioca and came out five million smackers ahead."

"Who is he anyway?" said Mr. Sahara.

"He's allegedly a public relations man for Mother Margolies' Activated Old World Chicken Soup, the brand served in our Noshorium," said Mr. Caesars Palace. "But I got some friends in a hush-hush bureau in DC. to check him out. The PR job is a cover. He's really Israeli Secret Agent Oy Oy Seven."

"I don't give a damn who he is," scowled Mr. Tropicana. "Question is do we take our losses and get scourged by our respective stockholders or try to recoup by challenging him at Monopoly? I personally favor going for broke."

A fervent chorus of "Me, too" cinched the decision for Mr. Caesars Palace. "OK, gents." He stuck a finger into the buzzer. The door opened and Lobsang Rampapport, sleek and self-assured, bade them enter.

"Mr. Bond knows why you are here, sirs. The Monopoly board is set up; the deeds have been waxed with Esquire neutral shoe polish; the houses and hotels given fresh coats of Sherwin-Williams paint. However, he insists upon two preconditions."

"Which are?" said a suspicious Mr. Dunes.

"First, he wants to use the silver doggie as his mover. He has loved the little doggie since childhood."

"Now, wait a damn minute!" roared the reddening Mr. Flamingo. "He's got one helluva nerve! I, too, always use the little doggie. I love the little doggie and—"

With an annoyed sigh Mr. Caesars Palace trod heavily on the point of Mr. Flamingo's Corfam brogue. "Agreed. Bond uses the doggie. But I get the race car, huh, fellas?" In deference to his role as host boniface, the other hotelmen nodded their sullen assent. "And the second precondition?"

Lobsang exhaled a contrail of Raleigh smoke. "He demands that the game be representational; that is to say, the hotels on the board will represent actual Fabulous Las Vegas real estate. In short, your hotels, sirs."

The moguls froze into attitudes of blinking incredulity.

"*Gottenu!* What *chutzpah!*" cried Mr. Caesars Palace. "He's out to turn the Strip into his private game preserve. Well, gents, there are eight movers, counting his, which means if we agree to function as a consortium the odds are seven to one in our favor. I say let's take him on."

"Still wish I was using the little doggie, though," said a rueful Mr. Flamingo, flicking a salty rillet from the corner of an eye, but he followed his colleagues across the parlor-pink Du Pont 1002 carpet (twice the thickness of the 501, which was not deemed luxuriant enough for a suite as splendiferous as the Maximus Rabinowus) into Bond's bedchamber.

Their target lay in a chinchilla hammock, a soigné hot-orange pair of Foster Grants masking his eyes and a provocative Mary Quant-type minijock barely concealing his wondrous underhang, viewing on a Zenith color TV the third game in a pro football tripleheader, the Runnerup Bowl, which pitted the loser of the NFL-AFL Superbowl against the winner of the NFL-AFL Super Runnerup Bowl. On a screen a commentator in an Armour's porkpie hat was saying, "... really hitting out there, Red. You can't tell me these guys don't take postseason football seriously when we've already had three definite deaths and eight maimings. 'Course, we did have our little moment of hilarity when the rabbit ran across the field, so let's have an instant NBC TV replay of the furry little fella's antics. Ah, there he goes! Notice how Br'er Rabbit seems to slow up just long enough to make the field judge commit himself, then runs a deep post pattern between Commissioner Rozelle and Sandra Dee. Our statistician, Larry Allen, tells me it's the third time in a Runnerup Bowl that a white rabbit has interrupted play. Brown rabbits have done it twice, of course. Any comments, Red?"

Via split-screen technique the announcer was joined by the Gallopin' Ghost telecasting from the Goodyear blimp.

"Well, Lindsay, it's been exciting from up here. The one development that's come as a surprise to me has been the Phila-delphia Eagles' usage of a seven-seven-eight pass defense."

"Course, that calls for twenty-two men, Red."

"Right! Oh, it's radical, no getting away from it, but darn effective. Murder on look-in passes, even when the look-in receiver has been guarded by a lookout. In general, though, I'd like to tell the fans what old 'Lonzo Stagg told me years ago: 'Red, keep your eyes on the field, 'cause in the long run that's where games are won or lost.'"

"Couldn't have said it better myself, Redhead. More pro action after this word from the all-new, all-charged-up Plymouth. Remember: *Plymouth is out to run you over this year....*"

"Mr. Bond, your opponents are here," announced Lobsang Rampapport.

Bond used his Zenith Space Command tuner to blow up the set, brushed a few burning shards from his sensual insteps and pulled himself into a sitting position. "I await your pleasure, gentlemen."

At 2:30 A.M. the impossible happend. Bond, on Connecticut Avenue and facing a staggering gauntlet of purple, orange and red properties, all with hotels, rolled his third consecutive boxcar to send him to the safety of JAIL for three turns, a throw that augured catastrophe for the Vegans. Mr. Desert Inn turned Rinso white as his snake-eyes deposited his top hat squarely on the Bond-owned, hotel-occupied Park Place and on the very next roll duplicated it to land on... Boardwalk! Then Mr. Stardust's racing car cruised to a CHANCE, his sweat-drenched fingers picked up the orange card and he came close to fainting as he read aloud its dictum: ADVANCE TO BOARDWALK.

It was all over; the consortium was bankrupt. "Quite by CHANCE," punned Mr. Caesars Palace in a noble display of wit in the face of utter defeat. One by one, the hotelmen walked over to Bond and piled the deeds to their empires in his hands.

"Vegas is yours, Mr. Bond," said Mr. Caesars Palace. "Those pieces of paper represent a few billion dollars in real estate, but they also mean thousands of jobs and the economy of an entire state. Keep Vegas humming, old man. As for me"—and Mr. Caesars Palace smiled bleakly—"it's back to selling National Shoes on Thursday nights and Saturdays until I can build up a stake big enough to take you on again."

Mr. Flamingo touched the victorious silver doggie to his lips. "Bye, little fella." His scalding tears dripped onto the Monopoly board, rusting out the Reading Railroad and short-circuiting Electric Company.

The crushed ex-owners had almost reached the corridor when Bond, his tone strained and husky, called out: "Take Vegas back! I don't want it. I want something else instead, something much bigger."

Mr. Sands spun on his heel, uncertainty and hope commingled in his expression. "What, Mr. Bond?"

Bond told them.

Mr. Caesars Palace disgustedly waved a pinky-ringed hand. "Forget it. Keep the damn hotels. Frank doesn't give private concerts in anybody's room at 3 in the morning."

"Wait!" Mr. Tropicana had grabbed Mr. Caesars Palace's lapels and aided by Mr. Aladdin was shoving him back into the suite. "You've got to ask him. Frank loves Vegas. He won't want to see his town go down the drain. Ask him, Mr. Caesars Palace, *ask* him..."

At 3 A.M. Caesars Palace exploded into mega-frenzy as the entertainment world's Chairman of the Board strolled through the main lobby, the sixty-piece Nelson Riddle orchestra at his heels.

At 3:05, the last warm-up A sounded, he held the hand-mike cockily and flashed a breezy grin at Bond and Lobsang. "Hi, Bonnie! How's your Clyde? We'll kick it off with 'My Kind Of Town,' segue into 'The Impossible Dream,' then..."

Bond's sensual jaw jutted out in belligerence. "You'll kick it off, *buddy boy*'—and the band quaked to hear someone laying down the law to the Chairman of the Board—"with 'Kick Out of You,' the exact arrangement from the *Songs for Young Lovers* LP; slide into 'What Makes the Sun Set?,' which I want done in *bossa nova* tempo; followed by 'There's No You,' "The Music Stopped,' (Bond rattled off thirteen more titles) and take out the set with 'Strangers in the Night.'" He stretched out on the hammock, rolling the little silver doggie around in his palm, an unnatural brilliance illuminating his darkly handsome profile.

He's going to crack, Lobsang thought; *he's going to crack. And I know just when and I can't stop it.* Though all of her three eyes were now raining torrents, she got hold of herself long enough to snap off the thin neck of a vial of Schloofen-22, the Service's powerful sedative, and inject a hypodermic needle into the cloudy solution.

Her prediction came to pass at the expected moment, the coda of "Strangers in the Night," when the Chairman of the

Board poured all of his brash tenderness into the phrase "dooby dooby doo."

From the hand of Israel Bond erupted a rifle-like crack. He looked dumbly into his palm, flecked with bits of silver and blood. "Oh, Lord, look what I've done! I've crushed the little silver doggie to atoms. The doggie's dead... Sarah's dead... it's all wrong, all wrong... dooby dooby doo..." and buried his heaving face in Lobsang's creamy decolletage.

"You may go, sir," she said to the balladeer. "You have saved Las Vegas, but broken a man's heart." After the room was cleared, she found a blue tributary on Bond's inner arm, slid in the hypo... and he knew temporary peace.

"Aleph priority!" Lobsang's frantic signal got her through to M. immediately. "M., it's all over for him. He's a lachrymose vegetable. It would rend your wonderful heart to see his face cloaked in five-o'clock shadow, maybe even a quarter to six." (In Jerusalem, M. shuddered.) "And he's been going about like a slob in that scruffy Sea Isle cotton shirt and black loafers. That kind of getup is permissible for third-rate British agents, not for Oy Oy Seven...."

"Dry all your eyes, Lobsang, my child." Even over the transcontinental cable M.'s voice conveyed its curative effect. "And take one of my proverbs of universal understanding to guide you in your hour of need: 'A man may work from sun to sun, but a woman's work has been so simplified by modern appliances it's too ridiculous to discuss.' *Shalom.*"

In the kitchen of the internationally renowned Ziggy's Restaurant, on Jerusalem's Bezalel Street, Mother Emma Esther Margolies —to the world, the creator of matchless chicken soup and philosophy; to a tiny coterie, M 33 and 1/3 of the Israeli Intelligence, M., Number One – ladled a pot of her Activated Old World Bessarabian Momma Ligga, the future of Oy Oy Seven weighing on her mind.

There were, to be sure, other pressing matters: the curious disappearance of the trawler, the resurgence of Nazism in Germany, threats from Egypt, Syria, Iran, and for some unexplained reason, Pitcairn Island, but the fate of Oy Oy Seven would be atop the agenda to be considered by Operations Chief Lazar Beame, her second in command; Z., the jocular, roly-polyish dead ringer for Harry Golden the tourists knew as restaurateur Ziggy Gershenfeld, and the new staff psychoanalyst, an American-

Jewish girl named Dr. Betty Freudan, whose book *Fulfill Your-self By Depriving Your Man* had caused a stir some years back. A gorgeous thing she was, too, M. thought. Why couldn't Oy Oy Seven fall for a girl like that instead of those empty-headed *shiksehs* who invariably brought him misery?

M. wasted no time as they filed in. "You should all look at the carbons of Neon Zion's report of Oy Oy Seven's first field assignment since that *gefailicheh** New York business."

> *TO: M.*
> *Subject: Oy Oy Seven*
>
> *At 22:10 hours on June 5, 1967 I accompanied Oy Oy Seven to a point designated on Map Gimmel-200 as Vector Herbert, from whence Syria's border raiders, El Shikourim,** have been harassing our farms and water projects. From the first I noticed several anomalies in his appearance. His Hammacher Schlemmer trenchcoat, which was in need of a pressing, had a wilted carnation in the buttonhole. There were three rents in his faded Levi Strauss night-stalking commando Levi's, also unpressed, and—this I feel is important—he was not wearing any of his famous five hundred pairs of stylish bedsocks. In his Neiman-Marcus shoulder holster, whose stench indicated it had not been saddle-soaped for ages, was no weapon, but a moldy Hebrew National salami. We did not motor to the border in his Mercedes Ben-Gurion, which I am told he has not driven since his last adventure. We went by cab. He did not overtip or even tip the driver. Instead he started a petty, vociferous squabble over the fare. I cautioned him, "Be still, Mr. Bond. El Shikourim may hear us." He grew surly and withdrawn, pulled out a Polaroid photo of the Lawrence woman, looked at it and wept.*
>
> *At 22:59 we crossed the marshes, our heads under water, breathing by the old hollow reed technique. Occasionally Oy Oy Seven would stop to blow bubbles. He seemed to think it amusing. Fortunately, some*

---

*   Terrible
** The Drinking Ones

braying donkeys on the Syrian side covered his puerile noises.

We lay in wait for El Shikourim about an hour under some scrub cacti and were rewarded by the sight of their red-bearded leader, Feisal Fullah-Sheik, a veteran terrorist suspected of killing several of our hydraulic engineers. During our vigil Oy Oy Seven had been drinking a very cheap, malodorous Turkish hair tonic (what a far cry from the glorious libations he ordered in the past!) and was disgustingly intoxicated. Instead of garroting the Syrian, he jumped up and shouted at the top of his lungs, "Feisal, baby! You wanna li'l taste?"

If his reason was absent, his storied luck was not. Feisal's mount, startled by the outburst, reared up and threw its rider headfirst into a wadi, where he incurred a broken neck. The other brigands, riding up to investigate the commotion, saw their leader expiring and fled in panic.

Oy Oy Seven examined the now dead Feisal and said, "I guess he got the point, eh, Zvi?"

This is the saddest part of my report. Of course, Zvi Gates, my predecessor as 113, licensed to wound, died in El Tiparillo two years ago. And the one-liner Mr. Bond threw at the corpse about getting "the point" would have been appropriate—if Feisal had been impaled by a harpoon gun or swordcane. *It lacks relevance when applied to a broken neck.*

My regretful conclusion: Israel Bond is no longer the world's most formidable secret agent, no longer the man I grew to worship in the Matzohball and Queen capers. Continuing him on as Oy Oy Seven would, I opine, jeopardize the entire operation of M 33 and 1/3 and his fellow agents and lower our prestige in global espionage circles.

Respectfully submitted,

—Neon Zion *(113)*

P.S. I want his Oy Oy Seven number.

A death ray from the planet Mongo could not have pierced the collective gloom, but Z. made a manful try. "The business about the bad joke young Zion puts so much emphasis on could be fixed, you know. Oy Oy Seven is mentally tired, that's all. The pressure of having to come up with a tremendous joke each time he kills has burned him out. A simple solution: We call up the William Morris show business agency in New York; they assign Jay Burton or Sheldon Keller to write Bond some fresh one-liners to cover any conceivable kind of death and—"

"That's no answer, Z, and you know it," snarled Op Chief Beame. "Neon's a nervy little *momser* asking for the world's most heralded license to kill, but he's right. Bond has had it. Hell, I've been puking at Rangemaster Rosenzweig's last few reports on Oy Oy Seven's shooting. He's been missing at three feet with a bazooka. The only thing he's hit in eight weeks is the late Rangemaster Rosenzweig."

A cluster of soup greens, which had been so crisp and lively, wilted at Beame's disclosure and fell with a disconsolate splash into a pot of chicken soup. M. pretended not to notice the mishap and said, "Dr. Freudan, may we hear the results of your psychiatric workup?"

The pert blonde crossed her splendid legs. "Before I recommended a Caesars Palace vacation for Oy Oy Seven I spent considerable time on his case. He is sound physically. The understandably severe injuries he suffered in the fall from the Empire State Building have healed in a satisfactory manner. However, he hallucinates whenever he has sexual intercourse. He sees the ghost of the veiled beauty, this Sarah Lawrence of Arabia he was to marry, standing over him, her accusatory eyes provoking great feelings of guilt."

M.'s withered face held a searching look. "How do you know he is physically sound, doctor?"

A blush stole over Dr. Freudan's cheeks. *Thank heaven I'm wearing an opaque skirt,* she thought. Her answer was a mite too defensive, she realized later. "I am a medical doctor as well, M., and I took it upon myself to examine Oy Oy Seven for any injuries that might be related to his mental state." *I couldn't help it,* her heart confessed. *There he was on the couch shivering so, the poor dear, so I covered him with a blanket, which didn't help, then my coat, my clothes, me, and then that* marvy musculature *was doing insane things to me—not the sweet semi-rape women are supposed to enjoy and really loathe, but pure and lovely bruising, bashing barbarity with the right touch of Neanderthal, plus a hint of Ervin Laventhal. Oh, Iz, Iz, my shameless love for you is branded on my face and M., the dear, sweet old wise thing, knows it!*

"You should do something about that burn on your face, Dr. Freudan," M. said with a cool, diagnostic smile. "An overdose of sun, hah? So, mine *tireh* doctor, what's to be done?" She, Z. and Beame awaited the summation that would close the door on the career of Israel Bond. From the damning evidence there could be no other verdict, it seemed.

Dr. Freudan lit a Raleigh. "In my researches into the qualities that make a secret agent the *rara avis*[*] that he is, I have learned one thing. When a secret agent appears to be down and out, unable to function in 'The Great Game,' it is a historical verity that he can be revived by the kind of intrigue and danger only to be found in Japan." *Oh, Iz, Iz,* she grieved inside. *I don't want to let you go, but it's the answer.*

Beame pounded his fist against the table. "You're crazier than Bond is. What the hell can Japan do for his breakdown? And why there? If you're thinking about putting him back into the field, let it be West Germany. Quiller didn't finish the job. Or Jordan. Let him knock off a few of these 'holy war in Palestine' nuts King Hussein can't control. Or let him check out a hare-brained story I just received to the effect that our missing trawler was seen going through the Suez Canal."

"It's got to be Japan." Dr. Freudan stared the op chief down. "Japan."

It was in M.'s lap, as all major decisions were, and they knew it. M. had these famous bees in her peruke, among them an exaggerated faith in agents who believed in dressing to kill to kill, whose parents came from the Ukrainian *shtetl* of Baronevkeh. Would she allow her prejudices to becloud her usual sound judgment?

"I'll tell you something a person learns only when she's in my eight-and-a-half-double-E low-heel I. Millers," M. said. "The Shinbet and Mossad have been jealous of our little agency's status for years and have been trying to convince the PM that we're unnecessary and should be incorporated into their

---

[*]   Or *rara hertz*. The usage depends on the latest ratings.

structure. One factor has kept M 33 and 1/3 autonomous—the incredible successes we've scored in the Loxfinger, Matzohball and Queen affairs, which have pulled our little nation from the abyss. And who, I should ask, is responsible for those successes? Oy Oy Seven, Israel Bond. If you all want to keep on picking up your paychecks you'll listen to me, *kinderlach*. So happens I agree with the good doctor."

Beame made a last stab. "Japan isn't even in our sphere of influence. There's nothing cooking for us in Japan."

M. clenched her gnarled fist and yelled, "Gnash! Gnash! Gnash! Gnash!"

"What's that supposed to mean?" asked Beame.

"I left mine teeth in a glass so it's the only way I can express my anger at your stupidity. If I know Oy Oy Seven, he'll start something cooking, don't worry. That lad could uncover suspense in a crate of lettuce. So it's settled. Z., you'll get Bond's friend in the CIA, Monroe Goshen, the fellow who got shot up in the Queen business, to send in Oy Oy Seven's behalf a nice letter of introduction to Baron Sanka, my counterpart in Tokyo. Beame, you'll prepare a white paper on the political situation in the Far East that Bond can use as reference material. I suggest you get in touch with the only truly knowledgeable people about that region, Sidney Toler or Warner Oland, who both played Charlie Chan. Dr. Freudan, you'll fly to Las Vegas and administer whatever therapy"—her tone was pointed—"he needs between now and departure time. Book him on Japan Air Lines, deluxe accommodations. A first-class killer should never fly tourist. And rehearse a hefty, hearty farewell for him at the airport. What is it the Japanese say? *Sy'n' Sarah*, no? My mind is made up. For the good of M 33 and 1/3, Eretz Israel and the whole profession of espionage, I decree: Send him to Japan!"

3

"Making Rove On Me—Fast! Fast!"

Somewhat dizzy from the bloodletting on the jet, Bond sagged against a wall of the Haneda Airport phone booth. "I got a bit of a break, Schlomo. Turns out that the Japan Air Lines purser who found me used to be the head surgeon at Kyoto General Hospital. He quit four days ago for the greater challenge of teaching Western air travelers the Japanese games of go and shogi. He rigged up a makeshift tubing by linking some soda straws and transfused me on the spot. Didn't have blood so he used Sacramento tomato juice. I can still hear the *plop, plop, plop* reverberating in my circulatory system."

On the other end, Schlomo Salvar, Bond's contact in the Israeli embassy, said, "I'd say it was *quite* a break, Oy Oy Seven. Damn glad to have you around. This idiocy concerning our trawler is causing repercussions. We've just been handed a stiff note from Count Iyama Pishaka of the Foreign Office. And the Sokka Datgai—that's the militant right-wing bunch—are threatening demonstrations against the 'warmongering Jews.' They've already burned down three USIS libraries."

"American libraries? Why?"

"We have none here. They've got to show their displeasure some way. Lucky thing you stopped that bogus monk or we'd also be liable for the loss of an eight-million-dollar jet, not to mention compensation to the passengers' relatives. One thing puzzles me. How did an Israeli ship ever sail blithely through Nasser's Big Ditch?"

"I don't know, Schlomo, but I do know our *Herr Doktor* is behind it. Keep Frequency Baze Tzaddik open at all times. I've got a Kral-Cain syncraphone hidden on me. *Shalom, Schlomo.*"

The two-way beeper, no larger than an Alka-Seltzer tablet, was concealed in the false sixth toe of his right Tasmanian Devil bedsock, a pair of which he'd slipped on before deplaning. He'd also donned tight-fitting Sebring Pit-Stop slacks and put on a happi coat and face. Tucked into his right-hand pocket was a snub-nose Simon-Garfunkel, the six-shot persuader tooled for him by gunmaker Paul Bines of Universal Firearms Corporation, the American firm that long ago had made an arrangement to furnish M 33 and 1/3 the latest in small arms in exchange for Raleigh coupons.

"Roses are red, violets are blue..."

"Sugar is sweet, but it's a damn good thing he retired from the ring; the kids were beginning to knock his block off."

The coded salutation came from a chubby New York type in the front seat of a boxy black Cedric sedan idling near the taxi stand. Bond replied, "Hickory dickory dock... The mouse ran up the clock... The clock struck one... The mouse got hysterical... He's now in rehab."

"You're my man," grinned the driver. "It's good to look on a *poonim* with a little *taam* in it.[*] My name's Heshy Burg from Mosholu Parkway. Baron Sanka sent me to pick you up. Since I'm always hanging around the main drag, the locals call me Ginza-Burg. Get in. I'll stow your gear in the back."

Though the Japanese custom is to drive on the left, the loquacious Ginza-Burg kept for the most part to the right lane of the freeway to Tokyo, sending oncoming motorist after oncoming motorist swerving into poles and abutments. "Hot damn!" chortled the ex-Bronxite. "Betcha I've sent almost fifty of the little buggers to their honorable ancestors." When he saw Bond's frown, he added hastily, "'Course, the government tacitly encourages this practice. Country's bursting at the seams. They're damn grateful if you help thin out the masses now and then."

During the pell-mell jaunt Bond learned Ginza-Burg was a Jackie Mason Rabbinical Seminary student who'd ranked high in his Talmudic studies, but flunked the major courses, Nightclub Standup Comedy 1 and 2. Embittered, he'd come to Japan in search of an "indefinable something." What it was he found hard to define, he admitted to Bond.

Ginza-Burg left the freeway at the turnoff to the Assakissa section and sped through a network of narrow alleys, halting in

---

[*]   A face with a little Jewish spirit

front of a two-story edifice at Ichiwada-ku, 4-chome, chrome-6. "We're here, Mr. Bond. Welcome to the Cathouse of the August Tea."

* * *

"Ichi! Ni! San!"

On *"san,"* Japanese for "three," the two men facing each other across the low lacquered black table unballed their right fists to reveal their choice of either one or two fingers in the age-old, intellectually demanding contest of odds-and-evens, played throughout the world and held in especial fondness by game-loving Orientals.

Each contestant jabbed out one finger.

"Evens!" An exultant cry escaped the throat of Baron Sanka, the chunky little man in the expensive *yukata* whose watercolor print depicted heroic kamikaze pilots diving their bomb-laden planes into West German camera and automobile factories. "Evens again, Izzy-san! My twelfth triumph in fifteen games."

Bond, sitting on a tatami mat in the cross-legged style of the East, knew he was playing badly. With just minimal concentration he might have been holding his own, perhaps even winning, because on Baron Sanka's playing hand there was only one finger.

To celebrate Sanka's win, the geisha Flowering Fungus let a hesitant smile play on her lips (her instinctive Eastern wisdom told her it was the correct anatomical location for such a display) and plucked a discordant tune from her six-stringed Selmer samisen, winning an approving *"Yo-I! Yo-I!"*[*] from Sanka and the madam of the pleasure palace, a shrewd-faced old woman named Eating the Mango.

"It is a very mournful air, Izzy-san," remarked the Baron. "I shall translate as she sings." As Flowering Fungus chanted in a wavering basso profundo, Sanka said, "It is the story of a great samurai, Raykko, which in English means 'Lord of the Auto Seat Cover.' One spring day Raykko wanders into a small village, where he is greeted by the headman and his wife. They present Raykko with fish and rice cakes and bow low. Presented with this unexpected opportunity, he swings his sword and decapitates them. The headman's son, Sardo, offers Raykko green tea and Raykko responds by cutting the boy in twain. He goes into each hut and chops up the sleeping inhabitants. A party of children back from an outing to Fuji approach and trill

---

*   Good! Good!

a gay song extolling the samurai's goodness. He runs amok and hacks them into mincemeat."

"I agree, Cocky," Bond said, using the diminutive form of Sanka's name. "It is a sad song."

"Oh, no, Izzy-san." Sanka registered mild shock. "To this point it has been a most jolly song, but now Flowering Fungus is singing the depressing part. Raykko looks about, but there is nobody left to kill. *Nobody.*" Was that a muffled sob from his host? "Think of it, my friend. Here is a warrior who has consecrated his life to the noble art of slaughter, and he stands there frustrated, no victims in sight. Oh, the final verse does tell us how he eviscerates a few cats, dogs and chickens, but it is just not the same."

The geisha's dirge was smothered by a raucous cacophony from an adjoining suite occupied by a group of American businessmen and the squawks of Billy Bones, a bleary-eyed parrot, who was the Cathouse of the August Tea's mascot: "Polly Adler wants a cracker—awk! Bless this house—awk! A Coorveh is not a Chevrolet—awk! Pieces of tail—awk!" *Friend parrot has been around,* Bond observed.

Eating the Mango showed her green and red waxed teeth in a smug grimace and chattered in Japanese to the Baron, who, laughed. *"Ah so des' ka!* Our honorable madam says the Yankees next door are complaining about her unreasonable price structure. She informs me she operates this house in accordance with a Western oil company slogan: 'You Expect More from American —And You Get It!' A droll comment, *hai?*"

"Dammit, Cocky!" The three Orientals were stunned as Bond brought his fist down on an irreplaceable Merciless Ming Dynasty vase, pulverizing it to smithereens. "Let's stop this hissing, bowing, *hai*ing, and *ahso*ing and get down to brass tacks. You know why I'm here. I want a piece of vital information from your organization so bad I can taste it, but I know damn well you won't give it to me until I prove my valor by locking horns with you in a battle of haiku poetry. That's the size of it, eh, Cocky?" Ashamed of his boorish tirade, Bond drove his fist into Eating the Mango's stomach in a sincere gesture of apology. At a sign from Sanka, Flowering Fungus bound Bond's mangled hand with cool mandarin orange peels, which possess blood-coagulating properties.

"Ah so des' ka, Izzy-san," said Sanka. "You have been boning up on our culture. Yes, haiku is the door to my confidence. As

you know, it is a unique form of poetic expression limited to seventeen syllables per verse. The only Western forms that have ever approached its feel, its nuances and shadings are the poems of Nick Kenny, in his Early Period, and the Burma-Shave rhymes so foolishly scorned by the Philistines of American belles lettres. Every Japanese, from the Emperor to the humblest *pachinko* ball polisher, is adept at haiku. Consider this verse by Karo, the seventeenth-century syrup manufacturer:

> *Only shrimp and eels*
> *can sate my hunger; O*
> *tempura! O morays!*

Does that not lift your heart, Izzy-san? No? Perhaps you would feel more at home with a contemporary haiku composed by the *baseboru* pitcher Masi Murakami, the only Japanese ever to have won a berth in the American big leagues, a bullpen job with the respected San Francisco Giants. Taste this instant of exquisite despair:

> *Woe! I hung a curve*
> *to Henry Aaron; they'll*
> *never find that mother!*

"Are you ready to enter the lists, Izzy-san?"

Bond's sensual nostrils fired a salvo of Raleigh smoke into a squadron of dragonflies on maneuvers around a lantern. One by one they fell dead into the courtyard pool. *Unleash your imagination, buddy boy,* he urged himself. *A good showing at haiku and Cocky-san will place his far-flung espionage network at your disposal. A bad one... well, don't even think about that.*

"Please accept this humble contribution to your art, Baron," Bond said and began to compose in a wobbly fashion.

> *"The gingko leaf, torn*
> *off by a breeze, falls, falls, falls,*
> *falls, falls, falls..."*

Gottenu! Fifteen syllables squandered and no meaningful resolution in sight. Think, Oy Oy Seven, think! A felicitous flash of creativity came to him and he had it.

"... and lands!"

Sanka's mouth widened; a mote of fear appeared in the
hitherto unrelenting eyes. *Good-o! Time to press home the advantage!*
Like a jaguar moving in for the kill, Bond hurled a second verse
at his shaken host.

> *"If 'seventeen' had*
> *seventeen syllables, this*
> *crap would be a snap!"*

"Superb!" breathed Sanka, applauding with his hand and
finger. Bond stubbed out his Raleigh on the Baron's big toe.
"Honesty compels me to admit the verse says nothing whatso-
ever "
"Then it is genuine haiku."
Emboldened by his successes, Bond chugalugged down a ten-
gallon container of sake. "Here's a bonus, Cocky-san, a sensible
Jewish rebuttal to an Anglo-Saxon's distorted viewpoint:

> *You only live twice? Feh!*
> *Fleming was wrong! You*
> *only live until you die!"*

Sanka, though entranced by this *gaijin's* hidden fires,
nevertheless said with mild severity, "It does not exactly fit the
pattern. Your verse is eighteen syllables. But I find the logic
incontestable. It would make an admirable book title."[*]
"Point of order, my dear Baron. What you just heard was
a Hebraic form called *chai-ku*, the *chai* being our symbol for
'eighteen,' thus permitting the use of *eighteen* syllables. Now to
business." Bond's cruelly handsome face assumed the animalistic
look feared by his enemies on seven continents, five oceans and,
by the latest Roper Poll, ninety-eight thousand lakes and forty-
three thousand reservoirs.
"Where is Dr. Ernst Holzknicht?"
The sentence lashed the room like an Arctic wind.
"I would be happy to give you a map showing the locations of
the Arab world's top-secret missile bases. Or a list of clandestine
anti-Zionist groups being bankrolled by rightist Texan billion-
aires."

---

[*]   I'll take it.—S.W.

"Where is Dr. Ernst Holzknicht?"

"Or Formula Pikadon Psi, our process for duplicating the Soviet's gigaton bomb at $39.95 per bomb. Or documents proving that the CIA is about to merge with the AFL-CIO."

"Where is Dr. Ernst Holzknicht?"

Baron Sanka looked away in chagrin and popped his thumb into his mouth.

"You don't know." Bond's words came out like leaden dumplings. "I broke my mental hump to master this haiku *narishkeit,*[*] and for what?" As quickly as it had come, the old-time combination of arrogance, tasteless humor and murder lust that had made Israel Bond the unparalleled engine of destruction he was faded away, and for a minute he lapsed into an embittered silence. "I knew this Japan mission was a sheer waste of time."

"I have dishonored our budding friendship. Flowering Fungus!" Sanka snapped a command and Bond saw the geisha blanch at the mention of a word—*seppuku.* She tiptoed to a closet and brought Sanka a huge sword.

"With this weapon," Sanka intoned, "I shall end my unworthy life. A simple crosscut from my left ankle to the right frontal lobe of my brain, then another from my navel to a spot precisely three inches above my left ear—"

"Stop!" Bond sent the sword flying out into the night with a backhanded swipe. There was a scream from the garden and a shout from one of the American businessmen: "Jesus! Somebody just killed Spotty Wassermann! Sixteen months I teach the *schmuck* to be a crackerjack Crackerjack salesman and he lets himself get bumped off by some gook."

Bond slammed the paper screen shut. "Suicide is no answer, Cocky. I want Holzknicht. I've told you about his handiwork, the murder of that sweet girl of yours on the plane, and though I can't prove it, it's drachmas to donuts he was behind that trawler deal. I want him. You're going to help me get him."

Sanka made a ceremonious bow. "I shall contact every single agent under my command, Izzy-san. However, there has been dishonor in this room tonight and only suicide can expunge its stain. Someone must die lest the gods be wrathful."

"You Japanese are really turned on by this suicide *shtick,* aren't you?"

"But of course. Dying is our way of life." Sanka wheeled suddenly, pointed a finger at Eating the Mango and Bond felt a

[*]   Foolishness

chill pass through him. *Gottenu!* The Baron was giving the hag a death sentence and she was bearing it with the stoicism of her breed. She bowed low and walked into the garden to retrieve the sword.

Sanka, sensing Bond's distaste, said indifferently, "What does it matter? She is old. Now some entertainment of a robust nature far more gratifying to a *gaijin* than unappreciated wisps of poetry, *hai?* Flowering Fungus is yours tonight. Do with her as you wish."

A great honor, Bond thought. *He is offering me his personal geisha. I cannot accept out of common decency. He is, after all, my host. And she is a dog.*

"I cannot allow you to go to your *futon*[*] alone, Baron. Are there others?"

"*Hai!*" Sanka clapped his meaty palms. "Send in the maidens!"

Through a side entrance undulated a river of pillow geishas, lithe and lissome, their eyes cast down in the charming modesty that befits a hooker. Bond's gray eyes cruised the line, then fixed on one who was tall, tan, young and lovely. "This one, Cocky-san."

She clasped her hands and bowed. "My name Ipanema."

Sanka leered. "You have chosen well, Izzy-san," he said and backed out of the room.

"You speak English, Ipanema?"

"Yiss. Spikking berry good Engrish."

Bond held the solemn, owl-eyed maiden to his breast. How weightless she was! "I'm so glad, my *goyischeh* geisha. I am a man touched by tragedy and only through such an encounter as we are about to experience can I feel the reawakening of spring. Can you appreciate the holiness of this moment in time?"

"Yiss. Spikking berry good Engrish."

She understands, she feels, his heart sang.

Her agile fingers unfastened his kimono, then hers, and they stood naked in a moonbeam. "You rooking at these hot cards, prease." She fanned out a deck of the notorious Yokohama Sex Shop playing cards, each illustrating one of the fifty-two positions of lovemaking. There was actually a fifty-third, the joker, which was quite unbelievable, he decided. *No man on earth could have deployed himself into that position. No six men!*

"You berry handsome man," she sighed, forcing him down upon a *futon* of indescribable softness, stuffed as it was with

[*]   Sleeping mat.

the throat feathers of eunuch hummingbirds. Then, without warning, she held him at arm's length. "Before I roving you is matter to discussing. Money."

Bond's heart fell. "So this everlasting 'rove' is predicated on commerciality?"

"Ten thousand, fifteen thousand, maybe twenty thousand yen." She could hold back her welling tears no longer. "Prease say you making rove on me, Izzy-san. Twenty thousand yen all I got."

Now Bond was weeping himself, acceptable, manly tears of a low salt content. "You sweet kid. Of course I'll do it. And not for twenty thousand or even fifteen. Ten's plenty, plus forty-five percent of your take, OK, baby?"

"Yiss. Now making rove on me, fast, fast!"

Their flanks came together in a fiery collision and as they knew each other carnally, the evanescent spectre of Sarah stood over his shoulder, the doleful eyes proclaiming: *I forgive you again, Iz, my darling, but do try to keep this sort of activity at a reasonable level, won't you?*

4
Tag Day
In Tokyo

He awoke to feel packets of thousand-yen notes thumping on his chest.

"Ipanema keeping her bargain, Izzy-san. As you sreeping I making many yen for you. Baron Sanka-san reaving this note."

It read: "I trust you are enjoying the favors of Ipanema. Later today I may have some news for you. Ginza-Burg waits below to drive you to the Tokyo Hilton—S."

In his Hilton suite an hour later Bond put the finishing touches on the questionnaire found in each folder of stationery. The usual pap: "Was your bellhop cheerful and courteous? Your chambermaid? The desk clerk? Were the meals tasty?" etc. After each query he wrote: "Disgusting," "Foul," "Swinish," and on the line designated for the guest's name scribbled a bold "Conrad Hilton." What a flap that would cause in the front office! Mass firings, morale problems, etc. Why was he engaging in this shabby cruelty so alien to his basic good nature? *Because you've been hurt,* answered his heart petulantly. *Now let somebody else, in this case a perfectly good, blameless hotel, know what suffering is!*

Sanka stopped by at 3 P.M. as Bond watched a Japanese salary man, the ubiquitous type in short-sleeved white shirt and black tie, step off the tenth-floor ledge of the adjacent Sanai-Flushai Building.

"*Gottenu!* Another suicide. Twelfth one I've witnessed since I checked in. Now, what was *his* terrible sin?"

Sanka shrugged. "Who knows? Perhaps he failed to obtain choice seats to the Kabuki for his employer. Or he might have knocked over the water cooler, which is unforgivable. At any rate, I have some information, Izzy-San."

Bond tensed, his long tapering fingers crushing a cast-iron water pitcher to paste in his anxiety. "Bravo, Cocky-san!"

"It is a small lead at best, but what is it you Westerners say— 'From little acorns come nutrition-starved oaks,' *hai?* One of my men, a fisherman named Nikko Tee-Yin, who possesses the well-known photographic mind, spotted a thug in the village of Shimonoshima, which is on Kyushu, our southernmost and warmest island. He cabled this morning that the man is a certain Skwato, a member of the despised midget people, the Pippu-Skweeku of northern Honshu."

"Why are they despised?"

"The majority of Japanese are short of stature. We must have somebody to look down to. The Pippu-Skweeku fill the bill ideally. Because of their size they make splendid undercover men. Our files show this particular one was a sub-subagent in Japan for the Terrorist Union for Suppressing Hebrews, which your evil doctor organized."

"Under what circumstances was he observed by your fisherman?"

"Skwato is attached to the retinue of a *gaijin*, a Danish archaeologist, Professor Igneous Feldspar, who has been carrying on some excavations in Shimonoshima. Feldspar has our blessing, of course, but we routinely plant a man among foreign visitors to assure that their enterprises are not inimical to our interests. Thus, Nikko Tee-Yin was assigned to the Feldspar party. Another fisherman more or less is never suspect in that territory. In the course of nosing about he came upon Skwato, who is helping the professor on his spelunking excursions into a labyrinth of caves even no Japanese has ever explored."

"This professor chap," said Bond, struggling to keep his demeanor bland. "What does he look like?"

Sanka heard Bond's hissing intake of air, saw the sensual lips pull back to expose the rich, red gums kept free of pyorrhea by five hundred Stim-U-Dent massages a day. He laughed. "I am way ahead of you, Izzy-san. You believe perhaps that Professor Feldspar and the hated Dr. Ernst Holzknicht are one and the same? I am sorry to disappoint you, but your description of Holzknicht as a man of medium height, with brown, 'almost sympathetic' eyes, close-cropped black hair and the large forehead of the scholar does not tally very well with this." He handed Bond a clipping from the Mainichi chain's English edition, banner-lined: THE GREAT DANE ARRIVES ON KYUSHU, SAYS

HE'LL DIG IT THE MOST! (*Cute line,* a jealous Bond thought.) Accompanying the lengthy article was a photograph taken at the airport in Beppu of a gigantic man with blond curls who must have stood at least seven feet and a sullen-eyed, thirtyish woman, lithe and leggy, whose fruitful charms burst every which way out of a topless hanky-kini. Bond knew that look, that of a woman sexually unfulfilled, who craved the bone-crushing foreplay, duringplay and let's-do-it-again-afterplay that only he, Israel Bond, could purvey.

"She is his wife, Magma, and they have been married just a short time. Their passports claim Danish citizenship and their credentials appear impeccable. But if you are willing to follow this slenderest of threads, Izzy-san, I shall be happy to accompany you to Kyushu, for by coincidence my next item of state business also takes me to the excavation site. In the same cable Nikko hinted that a discovery of the first rank has been made. On one of their expeditions deep into a cliff Feldspar and Skwato came across a series of scrolls, which Nikko overheard the former say are not inscribed in Japanese. Nikko asked the Dane to let him bring the scrolls to the surface, but Feldspar refused, claiming they have been hermetically sealed so long they might crumble to dust upon exposure to the elements. Nikko further said Feldspar and Skwato of late view him in a hostile light since it was presumptuous of a humble fisherman to make such a suggestion. It could be Nikko's cover is blown. Nevertheless, I want those scrolls in our government's hands. If they truly cannot be moved I shall have a portable Xerox machine brought to Shimonoshima and have them copied on the spot. Our next stop, Izzy-san, is the Xerox building, where"—the Baron's eyes danced—"a surprise awaits you. We go, *hai?*"

"*Hai,*" Bond said. *Hell, this lingo was duck soup if a guy applied himself a bit.*

The Israeli handcuffed to his wrist an attache case prepared for him months ago by Lavi HaLavi, the quartermaster of M 33 and 1/3 whose brilliant devices so often had saved Bond from death. *Pauvre* Lavi, thought Bond in French, the language he often used in contemplative moods. *Pauvre* Lavi, under treatment *encore* in Foam Rubber Acres, the service's rest *chez* for disturbed personnel, after another of his periodic bouts with madness. Lavi's latest whackout had come during the Queen show and at present he lay in Galilee crooning fados, those soulful Portuguese songs of unrequited love, and scribbling equations far beyond human comprehension, then airmailing them to mysterious addresses all over the globe. Because of his condition, the little QM had been unable to service Bond with the usual battery of espionage gimmicks. "You will have to go it alone this time," M. had phoned. "Your main weapon will be your brains," which comment had made Op Chief Beame laugh himself sick for twenty minutes.

Ginza-Burg's Cedric was at the hotel entrance and rocketed away on another round of Burg vs. the Japanese people, the twelve-toned *thonk, thonk, thonk* of human anatomies against fenders conducted in Leonard Bernstein fashion by the lone finger on Sanka's right hand.

"I can't contain my curiosity, Cocky," Bond confessed. "How did you end up with one finger? Karate accident?"

Sanka passed Bond a Hi-Lite cigarette. "This finger is the survivor of a rather painful episode dating back to World War Two."

"And what did you do in the great war, Daddy-san? Lead some bugle-blowing, doped-up banzai wave against the Yanks on Bataan?"

"Alas, no, Izzy-san. How worthy that would have been! I was far from the site of glorious carnage when hostilities broke out. Because of my proficiency in English I was placed in intelligence."

"I notice you have no problem with the letter *l*, which so many Japanese convert into *r*, as in the phrase rots of ruck.'"

"I am aware of the joke," Sanka said wryly. "It is *hirarious*. No, Izzy-san, the *l* is quite manageable. Hist! L-l-l-inda, l-l-l-ovely, l-l-l-ascivious, l-l-l-o-l-l-l-ipop. It is the *r* I sometimes have weal twouble pwonouncing. To continue, when the decision to bomb Pearl Harbor was made, I was a student at UCLA. As you know, all Japanese went to UCLA. During my stay there the student body consisted of 99.9 percent Japanese—all in intelligence and working in disguise as gardeners—and Jackie Robinson and Kenny Washington. After the attack, the FBI struck with frightening speed, interning every son of Dai Nippon save me."

"Why not you?"

"A great piece of luck. It so happened I was the house gardener of a film-studio press agent named Seymour Feig."

"Sy? Hey, he's an old buddy of mine."

"So? Well, Mr. Feig knew the authorities were coming for me so he negotiated a fast deal. I would be free in his custody if I agreed to play a series of spitting, gold-toothed Japanese villains in his company's war movies. I had no choice. It was that or spending years in a barbed-wire enclosure in the desert. Knocking out my teeth and replacing them with gold dentures, I tackled the job diligently, albeit it was simplified by the screen-writers, who gave me one line in each film: 'Fright Rootenant Armstrong, you 'Melican pig! Where is your aircraft carrier?' which I spoke to Van Johnson in *Rip the Nip!, Take That, Tojo!, Slap the Jap!* and similar extravaganzas. I was bayoneted by Van Johnson, strangled by Van Johnson, pushed into a pit of cobras by Van Johnson and in one film lost four fingers on this hand when an alleged dummy grenade went off. To this day, although I realize he is a most worthy thespian and was only following the scripts, *I hate Van Johnson."* The Baron's eyes were coals of fury. "Of course," Sanka added in a mitigating manner, "I hold no such dislike for Humphrey Bogart, who, as you know, did the bulk of his fighting in the European theater."

"You'll pardon my interruption of an intriguing narrative, Baron Sanka, but we're being tagged by someone who picked us up near the VIP Bar near Tokyo Tower."

"So?" said Sanka; a polite way of saying, "Pooh-pooh," Bond knew.

Bond pointed to Ginza-Burg's rear-view mirror. "Pink-and-orange two-seater, Kyushu license plates. Looks like a '67 Sony, one of those combination TV-set-and-car jobs I've seen around town. I see you're amused. This'll amuse you even more. It has no driver."

"But this is not possible, my impetuous friend." When Bond told him to see for himself, he said, *"Hai,* you are correct. Take a right turn at Tiger Tanaka Boulevard, Ginza-Burg, and we shall see if the tag stays on us."

"If we're being tagged by an agent being run by an adverse control," Bond said coolly, "we can do one of several things. One, we can lead the tag to a phony vector point. Two, we can get out of the car and make him tag us on foot. Three, we can flush and challenge him. Four, we can leave him unflushed and unchallenged, somehow contrive to get on *his* tail and tag *him*, hoping he'll lead us to his base. Five, we can lead him to a 'safe house,' 'mike' it, find out if he's working through a 'cutout' or a mailbox drop,' flush the 'cutout' and let the tag continue, unaware of the switch. Six, we can lead him into a waterfront dive, where he can do a one-and-a-half gainer."

"What the hell are you talking about?" yelled Sanka.

"That's real espionage patois," said a sheepish Bond. "I don't know what it means, either, but I thought the possibilities were worth exploring."

Ginza-Burg was on Tanaka Boulevard now, rolling past *sushi* shops, suntory bars and the Loew's Mikado, which was double-billing *Marat/Sato* and the prize-winning documentary *Hiroshima: Unspeakable Act of War or New Concept of Instant Urban Redevelopment?*

"The car is still with us," Sanka said. "Stop, Ginza-Burg."

The chauffeur braked the Cedric in front of a slanted-roof shrine dedicated to Frito, the ancient, beloved god of the corn chip. Bond looked back to find that the Sony also had halted, about a hundred feet behind. He lit a Raleigh and made a great show of relaxation designed to make their tag think they'd stopped for some social purpose.

Then his panther's body uncoiled, the pile-driver shoulders hit the side door, driving it off its hinges, and Bond was diving onto the bonnet of the Sony, his Simon-Garfunkel out and slamming its staccato *protest! protest! protest!* into the windscreen. The tiny auto was in reverse now, its wheels screaming under the burden of Bond's weight. *Dammit! Where was the driver?*

Gottenu! A gout of flame whizzed out from somewhere in the vehicle and—*thwack*—a slug lacerated its way through his happi coat into his right shoulder. He fell off the bonnet face down into the street, his enriched type-A claret spurting over the asphalt. Some drops seeped into a crack; a wayward seed was fertilized; a bunch of chrysanthemums popped up and grew to a foot in height.

Sanka and Ginza-Burg were out of the Cedric, the former shaking a futile finger at the disappearing Sony, the latter pulling Bond to his feet. "*Gevaldt!* You've been hit."

"Not really," Bond said mordantly. "The scab from my smallpox shot came off, that's all."

"You were right, Izzy-san," said a crestfallen Sanka. "I have been guilty of underestimating these people, whoever they are. What gall! Shadowing the Number One of the Japanese Secret Service in his own bailiwick!" He stammered the worst thing a Japanese can say about his own negligence. "*Shimatta!*"[*]

Bond's rejoinder was surly. "*No-shitta!*"[**]

---

[*]   I have made a gross blunder,
[**] You certainly have!

Score another one for the "oppo"!

5

"Forget About the Black Room!"

In the Nisei N' Nefu restaurant, one of countless little establishments tucked away in the basement arcades that criss-cross the Xerox Building, Sanka purchased enough mandarin orange peels to staunch Bond's newest wound. The Israeli, eager to try his hand at ordering native delicacies, took the restaurant owner out to the front window, which like so many Tokyo eateries contained plastic representations of the bill of fare, and leafing through *Instant Japanese,* the little booklet of basic terminology, pointed to *"this-su," "this-su"* and *"that-tu,"* his facile performance in the difficult tongue earning the man's respect. When they'd finished the repast, Bond rubbed his tummy. "I've been around, Baron, but I must admit I've never eaten better plastic."

They washed it down with frosty mugs of the soft drink preferred by 95 percent of Japan's parliament, Diet-Rite Cola, and took the elevator to the executive chambers of Xerox on the twentieth floor. Bond, a Raleigh between his sensual lips, mentally shredded the report he'd planned to send Mother Margolies' Activated Old World Products—or MOMAR, its cable designation. "I was shot up by a Buddhist bonze and a driverless car." How Neon, that cheeky little *putz*, would hoot at that one! "I told you Bond has gone crackers," he could hear Neon saying to M.— Neon Zion, whose life Bond twice had saved, and now the ungrateful punk was hungering for the Oy Oy Seven number, according to Betty Freudan, who'd leaked Bond the scam on the Jerusalem powwow. No, it would be far more sensible to inform the home office things were proceeding well and that he was Kyushu bound to track down a promising lead.

At the entrance to the Xerox suite Sanka winked. "That little surprise I mentioned waits inside, Izzy-san. But no matter what transpires, bring out that portable Xerox."

Bond's fist rocked the oaken door of the head Researchers suite, emblazoned with the Xerox motto: LET THE EMPLOYEES AT IBM THINK; YOU COPY.

A furry voice that sent desire pulsating through his lithe, muscular body said, "Come in."

She was bending over a worktable, her full lips pouting, her dazzling abel-green eyes poring over a complicated equation of five-dimensional multilinear galactic values arranged in conical plexigons of a base-ten, submicronite unit. Around her neck hung the silver chain and plunger that identified her as one of the ten members of MIT's most select scientific honor fraternity, Alta Zeyda Kapplan, which scorns any IQ under 355. The AZK frat-soror house, which carried out a humanitarian program of helping the handicapped, employed Mensa people as janitors and kitchen help, Bond knew.

The chain-and-plunger insignia was her lone concession to conventional garb. The rest of her was stark naked.

She did not appear in the least flustered by the gray eyes that toured her loosely coiffed ebony tresses, swan neck, muskmelon mammaries, awesome nether structure and rose-pink toes. *Gottenu! If the Japan Travel Bureau could guarantee regular tours like this, Europe would be deserted at the height of the season,* Bond thought.

"You must be the Mr. Bond the Baron telephoned about," she said in that provocative huskiness. "I am the head researcher here. My name is Kopy Katz."

Touché! Bond thought. How apt a name for a Xerox intellectual! What a specimen, the likes of which he'd never seen! And yet, would it do to start a love affair in a heart still haunted by Sarah?

"I'm no good for you." Bond said. "I'll take you, use you like a hot scented *oshibori* towel, then toss you into the wastebasket of broken dreams. You're looking at a man who has lost the capacity to love. I tell you all this because I possess ESP—Extra-Sexual Perception—and it's obvious to me you're longing to be violated."

"Maybe I am, maybe I'm not, Mr. Bond. Yes, I confess a sort of detached scientific interest in certain portions of your compelling body, but as for giving myself to a man I've known for less than thirty seconds, well..." Her speech ended on a brittle laugh.

Bond's right hand bludgeoned her face, leaving an angry five-fingered fan. "You bitches are all alike. You all want the little preliminaries to the game of love, don't you? Flowers, two-buck boxes of Whitman Samplers that I get at Korvette's for $1.59, friendship rings, juvenile kisses stolen on hayrides. Well, *ketzeleh*"—his cruelly handsome face stiffened, the last of him to do so—"here's a demonstration of what I can do for you, my insouciant Miss Kopy Katz. Take it or leave it."

Growling, he unlocked the attaché case from his wrist, removed the rolled-up movie screen and the alarm-clock-size projector, set them up and killed the lights. He sat back, crossed his legs and lit a Raleigh.

"THIS IS ISRAEL BOND" flashed on the screen, followed by an imaginative set of pop-art titles designed by Saul Bass, with scoring by Mancini. For the next five minutes the real scoring was Israel Bond's. The crisp narration by Doodles Weaver began:

"This is the story of Israel Bond, a man among men. Let's let vivacious Pennsylvania matron Charlene Krosnick, who often slips away from her husband and children to find unequaled bliss in Bond's arms, tell us part of it."

There was Charlene nibbling at his ear in his luxury suite in Manhattan's Ansonia Hotel. "Iz, Iz, Iz!" *Good opening sequence,* he thought. *Charlene always was an enthusiastic sort. Ah, a superbly executed Balinese three-quarter-angle stroke had made her swoon. Hope* that *melts the Mendenhall glacier in your innards, Miss Katz!*

Narrator: "And now a Catskill Mountain moment of madness..."

Mancini's musical mood was meringue; the love object Poontang Plenty; the place the Kahn-Tiki Hotel in Loch Sheldrake, New York. "Iz, Iz, Iz!" Watching Poontang's Revlon-tinted nails rip the heavy-duty Wilton carpet to tatters, he felt a pang echoing from the long ago. *Poontang, my sweet, lost love. Poontang...*

"Big-city love takes a back seat now to the kind o' down-home carryin' on in Amurrica's Midwest, as Omaha's cute-as-a-cornflower Katie Winters shows you in this silo scene." A square dance set the stage; the snub-nosed brunette snuggled on his shoulder. "Shucks, Iz. I've got a cool secret. I love yuh." *Dear little Katie Winters! If only she hadn't perspired so much.* The film rolled on.... Anna Annatefkeh, the voluptuous KGB killer in the spine-tingling Matzohball adventure, taken in *kazotsky* rhythm...

58   SOL WEINSTEIN

Liana Vine, his Trenton, New Jersey, high school sweetheart, succumbing to a *freilach*... Rowena Rosenthal, the teen-age "New Left" activist, joining him in a freakout to a Bob Dylan medley on a blanket made of *Ramparts* magazine covers (restless, restless Rowena! When the civil rights and peace movements had lost their spice for her, she'd moved to Mr. Rogers' neighborhood)... dozens of altar Bunnies yielding to him at Chicago's recently organized First Church of Hefner, Hedonist, under a stained-glass window depicting a frail, pipe-smoking man nailed to a circular bed: HE SWUNG TO MAKE US FREE... and, inevitably, Bond's conquest of Sarah Lawrence of Arabia on the moon-bathed dune. *Sarah, Sarah, my one true love...*

"Stop it! Stop it!" Kopy Katz's screams lancinated his eardrums.

He cut the film at the closing credit— PRODUCED BY R-K-OY PICTURES—and saw her sway against her desk. "I—I seem to sense the inchoate stirrings of a preorgasmic flush, Mr. Bond."

And he knew he had her on the ropes, helpless to ward off any onslaught. But wait! That mumbo jumbo she'd mouthed. Typical Masters-Johnson *Human Sexual Response* stuff. Of course! That was the key to copping a fast copulation from Kopy Katz, woman of science. He would woo her in her own frame of reference.

"Observe, Miss Katz," he said clinically. "My tumescence has become functional."

"Quite so, Mr. Bond," and her eyes confirmed his claim. "I myself have achieved a more than adequate state of lubricity accompanied by a pronounced vascocongestive increase in labial locations."

"Which would seem to call for immediate insertion of tumescence, Miss Katz."

"I should think so, yes, Mr. Bond. And please employ concomitant prestidigitation at crucial mons and clitoral checkpoints. Please."

They began a surging thrust that swept them rapidly past several preliminary plateau phases, the researcher moaning, "Manifest psychogenic reaction noted."

"Envelopment firm; friction mounting; all stimulative systems green," Bond reported.

"Oh, Mr. Bond! It behooves me to inform you that I'm veering at breakneck speed toward the arrival plateau. Oh, Iz, I'm arriving, arriving, arriving...."

"Quick! Join me in the Masters-Johnson cheer: Go, go, gonads! Go, go, gonads!"

But further jargon was unnecessary, for now his body was steering hers into the outer reaches of the universe, and she abandoned all diffidence and hotly whispered obscene spatial calculus into his ears during a "big bang" climax that melted innumerable Mars bars and intimidated Saturn into pawning four of its rings.

His own fulfillment was marred ever so slightly by the vision over his shoulder, who spoke through a tear-soaked veil. *Oh, Iz. You've been unfaithful again.*

I know, dearest, answered his cheating heart. *But I'm a man with a man's needs.*

"Iz." This voice was earthly. Kopy's. "I love you. But I ask no guarantees. Love me as long as you wish; then, if it pleases you, chuck me into that wastebasket."

Bond inhaled a Raleigh. "You think that portable doohickey can give us a clean reproduction of the scrolls?"

A lightning bolt fulminated out of the abel-green eyes. "You're damn tootin', buster! Xerox can copy anything, anything!"

Oh-oh. He'd hit a nerve ending there. Miss Katz appeared to be a real 150 percent, rah-rah "company" gal all the way.

"I see you don't believe me," she fumed. "Well, for your info, I've a project in a secret lab up here called the 'Black Room' where—" She bit her lip.

"What about the 'Black Room'?"

"Forget it, buster." Three word icicles. "Forget you ever heard me mention the 'Black Room.' Now, pick up that portable in the corner and let's get cracking."

6
Night of
Treemandous Terror

Deep in thought and Kopy, Bond, inhaling his 1,006th Raleigh of the day, lay in a compartment on the 150-mph blue-and-cream *Bullet,* the super-express train which has made Japan the talk of the transportation industry. Destination: Beppu, the place of the geysers, via Osaka, Kobe and the Inland Sea.

There'd been a piffling matter to dispose of before he'd checked out of the Hilton, a phone call from, of all people, blond, willowy Liana Vine, half a world away.

"Iz, darling. I've just been married here in Trenton at your brother Milton's catering house, the Pinochle Royale. I didn't want you to find out from anyone else."

"Who is he?" Bond had bellowed.

"A nice Jewish fella, Sidney Glumpkin. Owns a phylactery factory in the Williamsburg section of Brooklyn. I met him at the Concord on a ski weekend."

"Well, *slalom aleichem,*" Bond said rather nastily.

"Oh, Iz, don't take it that way, please. I was so lonely and I've waited two decades for your marriage proposal. I'm way past thirty, Iz. I need someone. There'll never be another you, especially at night, but..." Liana's voice dropped. He could hear the band striking up *Shereleh,* the vibrant wedding dance, disheartening proof that she indeed had taken the vows of a Jewish wife.

"And, Iz, I've long suspected you're some kind of a secret agent. So do your brothers, Milt and Rag Bond. Be careful, darling, please."

"Now, you listen to me, Liana. You've just done a sneaky little thing behind my back, but if you're married, you're married—that's it. However, I want you to swear you won't let this bumpkin or Glumpkin or whatever his name is touch you for a year. I'll know if you've lied to me, baby. The sin will eat through your face like leprosy. If at the end of the year you haven't heard from me, consummate the marriage with my blessings and name all the children after me. Israelita will do fine for the girl." She complied and he was appeased. "Now, put Glumpkin on. Sidney? You've just heard Liana's sacred pledge. Don't touch her, understand? Anyway, you'd be a fool to try and match the sexual pleasure I've been giving her all these years." He spent five minutes describing it in substantive detail to the groom. "And if I decide to marry her, you'll pay for the divorce, plus long-term alimony, right? Good. You sound like a decent clod, Glumpkin. Now go enjoy your married life." He hung up, proud of his equitable handling of the Liana situation.

But there were more important problems, anyway. That driverless-car business. Was it the beginning of a round of shadowings and attempts at assassination? If so, who was the target, Sanka or himself? Did the "oppo" know he was in Japan on a vengeful odyssey? This Danish egghead Feldspar—was he legit? Maybe, but why enlist the talents of a confirmed *pascudnyak* like Skwato? Or was Skwato using the professor as a cover for a new TUSH assault even more sinister than "Operation Alienation," which had decimated Israel's Secret Service and razed Mother's factory in Tel Aviv? Was Holzknicht in Japan or pulling the strings from long range? Questions, questions. Even this sweet kid in his arms had her secrets. That cryptic reference about the 'Black Room'... what was it all about?

There was a screech and Bond sailed headlong into a steel wall. "What the hell..."

Sanka strolled into his compartment and pressed a mandarin orange peel onto the knot mushrooming on Bond's temple. "Someone has jumped in front of the *Bullet,* Izzy-san, a common occurrence on this run. Some three million people per annum choose the railroads as their method of self-destruction. Not everyone has the stamina to climb up a volcano, you see."

"Suicide, suicide, suicide," Bond sighed.

"As I said previously, it is the time-honored way of expiating disgrace, and the more ingenious the suicide the more honor accrues to the victim's family. Here"—and the Baron handed Bond a newspaper. "This is the English edition of the Asahi chain. One of its most widely read features is the daily column of the witty Suicide Suzuki."

Surrounded by type was a half-column photo of one of the merriest faces Bond had ever beheld.

> *Hi, neighbor* [Bond read]. *Here's old SS on the neat, all-reet Death Beat! Hariko Harumi, the Sofia University dropout, also became a* dropoff *today— from the top of the Dream Center. Old hat, Hariko; wish I could say you've a second chance.... Yoshio Dai-Ichi is getting his kicks on the River Styx, and well-deserved ones, too, 'cause his departure was a thing of beauty. He went to Haneda and walked into a jet taxiing toward the terminal. Yup, it's the best when you die Northwest!... And let's hear it for Kono Yamato, who, having failed twice to cut out from this scene, finally worked it by cutting out himself. He flung himself under one of those machines at the Toyopet auto factory that stamps out parts from sheet metal. So, death wishers, if the grill of your next car has an extra-big grin, that's Kono....*

Death, death, death. Japan was a veritable discount house of it. Would his own sensual body be added to the pile before this caper was through?

He lounged on the *futon* and expelled a perfect smoke ring from his sensual lips, lined out two jets from his nostrils which crossed in midair to form an X, and watched the O and X float upward, the O taking a clear lead until it settled into the center of a ticktacktoe board he'd etched in the fluffy dust of the ceiling. Three O's across, game and set!

They had put up (and out) for the night at a Beppu *ryokan*, the type of inn where one sleeps on the floor of a sparsely furnished room. Kopy slumbered soundly, her arms locked in a protective, maternal way around the portable Xerox. Sanka had not seemed surprised that he and Kopy were sharing digs. "In Japan we do not yet possess your guilt concerning the cohabitation of unmarried people. We also place no stigma upon nudity, which is why Miss Katz feels free to walk our streets *au naturel.* Good night, my friend," and he'd retired to an adjoining room.

Bond extinguished his Raleigh in a porcelain bowl housing a delicate *ikebana* flower arrangement. A cunning breeze brought a shy daisy in contact with a randy azalea and he decorously looked away, though his ears caught the latter's imploring "I'm half crazy all for the love of you."

For a while he read the Good Book, then closed it midway through the story of Daniel. Tough spot that Daniel was in; Bond hoped he'd get out of that lion's den. Of course, if it had been written today Daniel would have a den mother in there with him. A wonderful book, the Bible. He read it every night— religiously.

There was a restiveness in him that precluded sleep. It was useless to fight that kind of feeling, so he opened the screen further and gazed into the garden with its oddly colored rocks, dwarf trees and a streamlet burbling its happiness at being alive and wet to the sultry full moon. As he tightened his lips around a Raleigh and scratched a blue-tipped Ohio match on the candy crystal of his Necco watch, the flare picked up a shadow.

One of the dwarf trees was moving.

He flipped the Raleigh away, cursing. Goddam cigarette was producing optical illusions now!

No, by thunder, the tree *was* moving!

There was a faint rustling as it picked its way past its partners, sidestepping rocks hither and thither, and then it braced and broad-jumped over the streamlet.

Bond's heart skipped a beat, then a whole twelve bars, for a sliver of moonlight illuminated something brandished by one of the fronds. *Gottenu!* A sugarcane bolo!

Across the garden toward the *ryokan* padded the tree, its steps almost inaudible on the thick tufts of gunter grass. Bond concealed himself in floor-length drapes, his incredulous gray eyes on the leafy stalker all the way. It brushed past him; he could smell the biting essence of its blossoms. Now it was poised outside the screen to Sanka's room.

Another fingery frond eased the screen along its track until it was almost completely open. The bolo was lifted high.

"Cocky! For God's sake, get up!"

There was a scream as the bolo sliced down, but Bond was already diving against the base of the trunk. His right shoulder bulled into the corrugated folds of the bark and he felt them cruelly abrade his flesh. His flying block drove the tree through a paper wall into another room and through the gash he could see its inhabitants spilled over the low tables. Sanka, his face contorted, was trying to stem with his finger a cascade of blood from a slash on his left shoulder that had laid it open to the bone. And now he was retreating in fear, for the dwarf tree was hurtling back, bolo cocked for the final coup.

Bond shouted another warning. "Cocky, duck!"

The bolo buzzed over Sanka's head like a giant gnat and Bond could hear a string of curses from somewhere inside the tree. *Gottenu!* How in heaven was he going to stop a rampaging killer tree?

The answer was on the wall, a glass partition containing a fire extinguisher and an ax. He hammered his fist into the case, wincing as the splinters bit into his knuckles, but he tugged the ax from its rack and swung it in a sweeping arc, grunting in satisfaction as its flat side caught the center of the dwarf tree in a crippling smash. There was a muffled cry; the tree spun around and lunged onto him and teeth were worrying at his shoulder, but the bites were feeble and did not pierce. Bond's left foot lanced out in a Pone Kingpetch kick, again catching the tree squarely in its middle, and he backed off, turned the ax around to expose the cutting edge and let go with the smooth, flat swing that he'd once used to fell a Sequoia. The edge bit in and the scream was a blood-curdling thing that trailed far out into the night. The tree split neatly in twain, a bloodbath burst through the bark and the halves lay still.

"Iz!" Kopy, pale as an uncoated Creamsicle, rolled into the Baron's room on rubber legs, stared at the ghastly remains at Bond's feet and swooned. He let her slide softly to the tatami mat.

"I need a doctor, Izzy-san. Badly."

Bond's alert eyes told him Sanka would bleed to death if not tended to posthaste. *Gottenu!* His kingdom for a tube of the cherry salve that could halt the flow in a second! Or a dozen mandarin orange peels!

Wait! The old Celanese tobacco trick taught to him by Sir Hu Wu Wu Herbert, the head of Ceylon's secret service; would it work on such a grievous wound?

He dashed to his room and took a carton of Raleighs from his luggage and a bullet from the chamber of his Simon-Garfunkel.

"Cocky, bite hard on this," he snapped, inserting the slug between the Baron's gold teeth.

"How will biting on the bullet help?"

"You always bite on a bullet when someone's dressing your wound. It's tradition. Besides, if you swallow it, it makes excellent roughage, I daresay."

Bond field-stripped two hundred cigarettes and jammed the tobacco into the raw fissure, tamping it down with the ax handle. Sanka grimaced several times but bore the ordeal with the courage of his race.

The gushing slowed to a trickle, then stopped.

They exchanged smiles, two spymasters who genuinely appreciated each other's manliness in the face of peril.

Bond let go a sigh as he first began to feel the injury he himself had incurred when his shoulder rammed the abrasive covering on the dwarf tree. "I'll say this." He grinned. "His bark was worse than his bite." *(Great one-liner,* his brain told him. *You're not ready for the trash heap yet, my friend!)*

Sanka was on his knees beside the tree halves, his nimble finger stripping away the husk and fronds. "I regret I did not have the presence of mind to say, 'Landsman, spare that tree!' Izzy-san. We might have learned something important if we'd kept it alive." He gave a low whistle. "By the belly of Buddha! Look what lurked under this camouflage!"

It was the severed body of a man, which, if joined, could have been no more than two feet tall. Even in the rictus of death the teeth continued to grind in the slavering mouth; the eyes remained pools of unspeakable ferocity.

"Without doubt, Izzy-san"—and Sanka's nose wrinkled in disgust—"this ugly little night crawler is the thug described by Nikko Tee-Yin. Yes, my *gaijin* friend, you are looking at Skwato."

7
Fisherman
Overboard!

Sanka, fully revivified, set upon the trail of the marauder, his keen eyes questing over the garden, picking up a telltale spot of crushed grass here, a bent twig there. "There is an old saying by a sixteenth-century animal tracker: 'It is easier to follow the spoor of a lion than that of a flea.'"

Bond nodded in acknowledgment of the wisdom, which came close to equaling M.'s.

A mile down the road parked under a banyan tree was the Sony. Bond plucked a banyana from a low-hanging branch, peeled off its yellow skin and munched away while Sanka conjectured.

"Now we know why we could not see the driver, Izzy-san. Skwato was so short he operated the vehicle from under the windscreen. If I am not mistaken there is some sort of periscopic device which enabled him to see the roadway and an aperture through which he put that bullet into you. The dwarf tree disguise is an old Pippu-Skweeku one for practicing the art of a *ninja* or a 'stealer-in' to commit murder. Other members of his clan have hidden themselves in umbrella stands and bowling bags. He probably shadowed us to Tokyo Station, learned our destination and drove to the Inland Sea, where he brought his car over by ferry, perhaps the very one we used."

"One thing disturbs me, Cocky. His target was you. Someone does not wish your presence at Shimonoshima. Feldspar?"

"Who knows? Let us waste no time in finding out."

On the 175-kilometer junket to Shimonoshima by rented limousine, Sanka was meditative. In the back seat, Kopy, still unnerved by the bizarre, bloody incident, held Bond to her heart.

"Iz, I've a feeling you're an Israeli secret agent. I know what Sanka's profession is and if you're chummy with him you're in the same game. Oh, angel, I came so close to losing you. A man like you has his head on the chopping block every second of his life. Maybe the next time you won't be so lucky. If I ever get you back to Tokyo alive... the 'Black Room'... yes, the 'Black Room.'"

He saw she had been wrestling with a monumental decision and patently had made it.

The air became rarefied as the vehicle climbed the road winding around a range of cliffs, rumbled through jungle terrain and past exploding *jigoku,* the "hells," which sprayed a gaudy variety of colored boiling plumes into the mist from the nearby sea. At the top of the tallest cliff they came upon a sprawling tent city, the headquarters of the Feldspar expedition, Bond presumed. They made a bumpy stop near the largest tent. "Feldspar-san," the driver said.

A massive hand covered with golden hair pushed aside a flap and the seven-foot Igneous Feldspar, ducking his head so he could ease himself out, emerged and wobbled toward them on giraffe legs.

"My dear Baron Sanka." His hand smothered the Baron's. "How good of you to have come." Ice-blue eyes in a pasty face snapped photos of Bond and Kopy. "I am afraid I have not had the pleasure of meeting these people."

"My name is Israel Bond." Bond watched for a reaction that never came. "A friend of the Baron's. And this is Miss Kopy Katz, who's come to Xerox your scrolls."

"Excellent! I had not wished to make a bothersome issue out of the scrolls, but until I can devise some safe way of bringing them to the surface I must insist they remain in the cave."

Sanka lit a Shinsei. "*Yo-i!* Then that is settled." He held something under the giant's nose. "Professor, look at this photograph. I took it in a Beppu *ryokan* moments after the subject tried to assassinate me. Do you know this man?"

"Why, it is Skwato, the little drifter I met here during the early days of my excavations, a foul-tempered, friendless being, but I took pity upon him and gave him employment. His size permitted him to squeeze into tiny crevices in search of fossils, and on one of these excursions he found the scrolls. He tried to kill you, you say?"

"Yes, but Mr. Bond thwarted the attempt. Skwato is dead."

"Then we all owe you a great debt, Mr. Bond," said the giant, shaking his blond curls in disbelief. "Ah, it seems this expedition is cursed. Skwato is the second of my workmen to meet a violent end."

Sanka's finger whirled in agitation. "The second?"

"A dreadful misfortune took the life of one of the men who supply us daily with fresh seafood. Standing too close to the edge of the cliff, he was caught by one of the unpredictable air currents that swirl between the cliffs and the ocean. He toppled one thousand feet."

"Who was this fisherman?"

"A man called Nikko Tee-Yin."

8
A Crawler,
a Baller

Dinner, held out of doors and served by taciturn Japanese, was a subdued affair despite the excellence of the professor's cuisine. Bond had never tasted anything as succulent as the Da Nang pongi stake shoots doused in the Green Giant's delicately seasoned butter sauce and Camembert Kampfert cheese dip.

Sanka was unaffable, no doubt brooding over the "accident" that had cost him a first-rate *tantei*,[*] Bond thought. Who had been the convenient "air current"? Feldspar? Or one of his many aides, including some Scandinavians in long-sleeved black sweaters not given to much more than some noncommittal small talk and a hawk-faced man who spoke English in a thick Slavic accent. He'd been introduced by Feldspar as Dr. Yaynu, a Bulgarian paleontologist who'd quit his homeland before the Communist takeover.

Bond, resplendent in Takashima cultured-pearl pajamas and Alfie bedsocks which had cost him thirty quid and six buskers, quaffed his fifth flagon of Beefeater Gin and coleslaw. "Where, professor, is the charming Mrs. Feldspar? I've not seen her since we arrived," queried Bond, and he got a jealous stare from Kopy that would have snuffed out a wildcat oil fire. She dashed her *patie de marco* lungfish soufflé into his face and exited in tears.

"Magma has asked to be excused, Mr. Bond. She finds these humid Kyushu nights too taxing. Indeed, all of Japan bores her, I fear. Perhaps she will prove more companionable on the morrow. I myself have come to adore this land. Here is a sense of order and harmony I find lacking in decadent Europe and its preoccupation with television, go-go girls, *le hot dog* and the

---

[*] Spy

scandalous behavior of the jet set. I have searched my heart for a way to repay Japan for the serenity she has brought me and I think I have found it."

"But certainly the discovery of the scrolls is repayment enough."

"That is a contribution to the world, Mr. Bond, and, incidentally, tomorrow I shall reveal a portion of the scrolls' contents at an international press conference to which you are cordially invited. Working in the cave by dim kerosene lamplight, I was only able to jot down a few paragraphs, which I have transcribed into English. My gift to Japan is of a more personal nature. At my own expense I shall rebuild the Great Herrosukka Buddha, whose ruins lie a few hundred yards from the main cave."

Bond sensed the fervor in Feldspar, a man with a mission— one of construction, not destruction, as Bond's was—and for a moment the Israeli felt ashamed at his years in the seamy spy business. The Dane seemed a likable, openhearted chap and Bond hoped he was an innocent party in this affair.

"The Great Herrosukka Buddha, Mr. Bond, was literally the idol of millions of Kyushu Japanese. On holy days throngs made their way up these cliffs, some on foot, the elderly on donkeys, to place garlands of onion rings at its feet and burn joss sticks of Wrigley's seaweed gum. Then a year ago a typhoon of extraordinary magnitude struck, flattening thousands of homes, killing hundreds of thousands of peasants, destroying the sisal and jute crops, which are the staple diet of Kyushu farmers. It climaxed its assault by hurling the Buddha into the Pacific, leaving only the tattered base. The Norwegians whom you met this evening are construction experts and, indeed, one of them, Ibsen, holds the rank of Master Builder. Working from my sketch of the Buddha, they will reconstruct it in a matter of days until it again towers one hundred feet into the sky of Japan. Then will my debt be repaid. And now I shall retire to my tent to burn the midnight oil over my scroll translations. Goodnight, Mr. Bond."

Feldspar bowed and stumbled off on the giraffe legs. *Poor bastard,* Bond thought. *It's as though he were on stilts.*

Stilts!

By thunder, he'd been a maudlin fool.

There was a quick way to find out. His long, tapering fingers yanked the Bowie-Handicapper throwing knife from his right bedsock and zipped it at the departing scientist. Feldspar yelped as the tip bit into his left calf, tripped and fell over a hibachi stove, howling again as a sleeve of his Ruark bush jacket caught fire.

Bond snatched the bowl of cheese dip and used it to quench the flames. "Professor, a thousand pardons. I had to do it. I thought somehow you were Dr. Ernst Holzknicht."

"Holzknicht!" The Dane's face whitened in loathing.

"Holzknicht!" Clamping his steam shovel of a hand against his leg, he hopped into his tent and closed the flap.

That's torn it, Bond thought. *I've just knifed my host on a ridiculous, billion-to-one-shot. The man must think I'm a mindless butcher. Yet how horrified he was when I dropped the magic name. Could be my nemesis has a hold on him. You're getting into deep waters, my friend.*

On the way to his tent, some five yards from Kopy's, he heard her wind-borne sobs. Hell, another jealous broad. Just because you balled 'em and promised undying love, they thought they owned you. Let her stew a bit.

His lodging was no Imperial Hotel suite, that was certain. A cot, a blanket, a fifty-yen reproduction of the *Mona Lisa* tacked over his pillow. A sardonic smile curved his sensual mouth. Didn't they think he knew that under the *Mona Lisa's* moustache was an enigmatic smile, not an O-shaped expression? Who did they think they were fooling with, some M.I. 6 idiot? Sure enough, inside the O was the little electronic snooper, a Reddy Kilowatt bug with a Dr. Seuss-Ikon frequency range of six long-ton hectares, a standard piece of TUSH equipment. Who was the patient listener on the other end?

He ground it to jonesereens under his contemptuous heel, stripped to his E. J. Korvette parsely-patterned wallaby-skin skivvies and stretched out on the cot. From his bag he took a gallon of Suntory, the excellent Japanese Scotch, poured it into a water bucket, mixed in shredded ginger, soy sauce and a pinch of Mother Margolies' Activated Old World *lekvar* and guzzled it down. He blew out the candle, pulled up the blanket and in seconds was dreaming he was locked in a backstage room at the Copacabana, the entire chorus line begging for his sexual favors. *Well, the show must go on,* he jested in his sleep.

Something woke him.

Something on his ankle.

Israel Bond froze. Tendrils were moving up his right leg, parting the fine, grade A-1 hairs covering the blemish-free epidermis he toned each day with brisk Dannon yogurt rubs. *Don't move a furge of a fifkin, Oy Oy Seven,* his brain told him. It may be the lethal Kyushu tarantula! Or the golden Ibusuki scorpion, whose sting... Don't move a muscle! The tendrils had passed the knees he'd studiously had recapped every twenty thousand miles and were gliding toward his inner thigh, higher and higher. *Gottenu!* What if it was headed... there? And it was, dammit, it was! He couldn't let it vitiate his manhood; he couldn't....

His right hand slammed down, mashed something and there was a splintering noise and a stifled scream.

"My hand, you've broken my hand...."

He fished an Ohio blue-tipped match from his Takashimas and relit the candle.

His nocturnal visitor was a naked woman!

9
Kopy Enraged,
Kopy Engaged

Magma Feldspar, the tigerish blonde whose sex-starved face had hungered for him from the newspaper clipping, writhed like a ferret in the steel trap of his hand. "I've been watching you all day through binoculars," she whispered. "I didn't dare greet you at dinner because I think I'd have torn the pj's off your lithe, muscular body then and there. For the love of Eros or any other banned magazine, take me, take me, take me!"

He released her hand. "Let's not be puerile about it, baby. A situation like this calls for a little savoir faire." On his compact Webcor he placed a spool of tasteful recordings he often used to make love by. His gray eyes sparkled a teasing challenge. "What'll it be? *The Friggin Forkful? The Muggers and the Fuggers? Swing Along with Mitch? George Beverly Shea Sings for Fundamentalist Lovers? Hava Negila?*"

"If a *negila* is what I think it is, yes, I'll hava *negila!* And you, you hava piece of Danish now!"

He sprinkled a pint jar of Nescafé on her glistening flesh (it was unthinkable to have Danish without coffee) and released the unbearable tension in her, saving the red-corpuscle-melting Siberian Steppe backflip for the joint moment of cataclysmic unification.

Sarah's face floated above him, her sloe eyes two leaky faucets. *Oh, Iz, Iz! Again?*

Forgive me, angel, but I'm a man, etc.

Thwick! Thwack! Two flashes of pain flayed his back and he whirled to find Kopy wielding a belt. "You-you rotten..." She could not finish her recriminations, choked on the tears streaming into her mouth and ran blindly into the night.

Magma lit a Raleigh. "You seem to be in demand, my Sinai stud. I don't care as long as I get my share."

Bond poured her fifteen fingers of Suntory and watched her toss it down like a dockhand. Fun time was over. Now the snap quiz. "How did you ever tie the knot with our nonswinging seven-footer? You don't look like the ivory-tower type, Mag. The basement is more your speed."

Magma threw back her hustler's head and cackled. "You've got me pegged, Bond. Iggie bores the hell out of me. I met him in Copenhagen a few months ago when I was a bar girl at the Club Elsinore. He took a shine to me, came in night after night, spent *mucho dinero*. Then he popped the question and I said to myself, 'Magma, you're not getting any younger,' so I accepted. The question was the last thing he's ever popped."

Bond ran his hand over her quivering navel. "Tough situation for a gal with your appetite."

"You said it, handsome. Hell, when I realized he wasn't going to do anything more than kiss me good night on the cheek and mess with his books and formulae, I decided I'd have to catch a little extracurricular jazz now and then. But none of 'em have been anything like tonight. Why all the questions? You some kind of secret agent?"

"Has he ever mentioned the name Ernst Holzknicht?"

Magma sat up, her mouth in a hard line. "I've answered all I'm going to. Sleep tight, tiger."

Bond bent her head with a slap. "And you've had your last tankful, Mag, unless..."

"All right, all right." She gingerly touched her swelling cheek. "Once Iggie got a long-distance call. We were in West Berlin at the time. He turned pale, started to shake. I heard him say, 'Ernst, for God's sake don't hurt the boy. I'll comply.' Shortly thereafter, Iggie said we were coming to Japan. That's all I know; I swear it."

"Toodle-oo, Magma. We'll have some more hanky-panky in your tanky real soon." He kicked her out, lit a Raleigh and reviewed the tidbits she'd contributed. The pieces of the puzzle were coming together. Holzknicht did have a hold on the giant— "the boy," whoever he was. He'd have to win the Dane's confidence and perhaps do Feldspar a good turn before this caper was ended.

Deep racking sobs rent the air. Kopy. He'd treated her pretty rough, he supposed. Time to make up. He crept into her tent and embraced the puffy-eyed researcher.

"Oh, Iz, how could you hurt me so?"

Bond stroked the ebony tresses. "It was strictly in the line of duty, *maideleh*. Remember what you said about a secret agent facing death every second? Well, what you just saw was a perfect illustration. I could have died of ecstasy from what that broad was doing to me."

Her lips were two raspberry floats brushing his neck. "Darling, you don't know how difficult it is for a nice Jewish girl. We'd all like to marry our own kind of fellas, but you Jewish boys treat us so mean. You see a Jewish girl and right away you run a mental Dun and Bradstreet on her. Is she pretty? Accomplished? Rich? Then along comes a heavy-breathing *shikseh* like that Magma and all of a sudden it's *love* with no questions asked."

"*Are* you rich?" He hoped the query sounded lighthearted.

"Heavens, yes. An Alta Zeydah Kapplan won't touch a job under one hundred thou' per. And Daddy's loaded. Made a pile pushing a line of low-cholesterol, high-protein foods—organic swamp cabbage, newt burgers, tumbleweed tea. Surely you've heard of him—'Unsaturated' Katz?"

"You bet," and his hand was sliding the nearly tenth-of-a-carat garnet engagement ring onto her third finger left hand. "You and I are for keeps, Kopy Katz. Hit Xerox for a raise. Little squeakers need tons of white booties and nappies."

Deliriously happy, she fell into his bronzed arms. "Oh, Iz! Iz!" Then slyly, "Do you think you can instigate another state of tumescence?"

Bond grinned. "I guess it can be arranged, luv." To himself: *Gottenu! In the near future I damn well better get to the first sperm bank I can find, and make a withdrawal!*

10
Shimon
Sez

The Dane's aides had set up a long press table outside his tent for representatives of every leading TV network, newspaper, wire service and news magazine, plus correspondents from *Women's Wear Daily, The Boot & Shoe Recorder, Fact, Playboy* and *Variety*. At each place setting was a pitcher of Yoo-Hoo chocolate drink and two Mallomars. Clarence Petersen, the *Chicago Tribune's* man, nibbled his and spoke to Norman Shavin of the *Atlanta Constitution*. "Better be damn good to drag us out to this Godforsaken place. Probably some third-rate fossil find worth two graphs on the split page of the *Moline Dispatch*. Nothing's going to knock that trawler story off page one, anyway. Wonder what got into the Israelis? They've got enough trouble with the fezzes without stirring up Japan's litchi nuts."

"Yeah." Shavin nodded. "I hear the Sokka Datgai is picketing Ann Dinken's Kosher-style Restaurant and the Tokyo Jewish Community Center with signs—YIDDEN GAY AHAME. Here's Feldspar. Lord, what a long drink of water!"

Igneous Feldspar lurched on the giraffe legs to the head of the table. "Ladies and gentlemen, it was gracious of you to make this rugged voyage to an obscure village. When I have concluded my presentation I am sure you will feel it was worth the effort. I have in my hands a few golden gems of a historical treasure trove, the translated excerpts of scrolls discovered in these cliffs by my associates and myself. To preface my remarks, let me say that we are all derived from one of four major strains, Negroid, Caucasoid, Mongoloid and Trapezoid."

The CBS-TV news chief puffed his pipe. "Trapezoid? I must admit, Professor Feldspar, that the last-named group is quite unfamiliar to me, perhaps even to all of us gathered here in this strange moonscape of a setting, wondering what astonishing developments await us on this muggy day in the twentieth century, sponsored, as you know, by the Prudential Insurance Company, whose public-affairs television documentaries have—"

"Knock it off, Walter!" expostulated his curly-haired, boyish NBC-TV rival. "You still haven't learned. To keep your sentences. Terse and punchy."

"Bring back Arnold Zenker," said the other NBC-TV man.

"The Trapezoids," said Feldspar, "flourished millions of years ago and were so named because of their unusual shape. They are now extinct. Because of that shape they were unable to enter restaurant doors and thus perished of starvation. What I am leading up to is that one would have expected these scrolls to have been written in the ideographs of the Mongoloid peoples who came to Japan from the great Asian continent. They are not."

Dozens of eyebrows rose.

"No, the scrolls are not Oriental. In point of fact, they are written on papyrus."

Shavin nudged Petersen's arm. "Papyrus? Hell, that's Middle Eastern. The Nips use rice paper."

Feldspar smiled. "Correct. These scrolls are an admixture of Aramaic and Hebrew. They are the work of a diarist named Shimon, who appears to have begun recording his experiences sometime between 800 and 700 B.C., about the time the Assyrians were bidding to dominate the known world. In some of the scrolls, which I've bypassed for the sake of brevity, Shimon tells of towns being sacked by the armies of Sargon II. I shall begin where Shimon, his wife, Rachel, and their infant son, Zoomgolli, and others of their clan decide to leave the region.

SCROLL FOUR

Shambles! Dispersed by the invader, Israel is no more. Ruben the Soothsayer, seeking a sign from the Lord of Hosts, came to our tent at the instant tiny Zoomgolli spake his first word. It was not the typical cooing attempt at "mother" or "father." It was distinct—"East."

Ruben says the divine summons has been sent to us through the child. We shall go east!

SCROLL NINE

Weary of body and soul, stardust and moonglow, wine and roses, we paused to seek shelter in a village of crude huts. The inhabitants, a listless lot, sit in the sun performing some profane invocation to false gods by pressing to their lips tubes of an acrid weed whose tips have been lit by fire, then drawing the smoke into their lungs. Rachel, whose olfactory sense is keen, said, "What a mess o' pot!"

Feldspar pounded the table. "Gentlemen, can you not see the woman's random comment, altered a trifle by succeeding generations, has come down to us as... Mesopotamia?"

SCROLL TEN

I am one hundred years old today. To mark the occasion sweet Rachel baked a cheesecake from a secret formula taught her by Sarah and Leah, matriarchs of the tribe of Gad. Someday, I predict, the Sarah-Leah cheesecake will be a delectation to all mankind. Zoomgolli does not share our festivity. He remains a solemn, introspective boy of ten and has not uttered a single word since the one that impelled us onward. Does he await a new command from on high?

SCROLL ELEVEN

The word has come! Zoomgolli cried, "East!" Zebediah the Kohan [high priest] said, "Let it be done." Tonight we trek east.

"Many did not survive the march through the land of the Medes we know as Iran," noted Feldspar. "Shimon cites his increasing age; he is now one hundred and fifty, Rachel ten years younger. Zoomgolli, sixty, remains reticent. He cannot hear well, Shimon says, because of his habit of stuffing dead birds in his ears."

SCROLL NINETEEN

We are in a barren land of scorching deserts, whose denizens are sly of face, sinewy of body.

They ride horses and camels like *mishigoyim*, swooping down on our encampment to pillage and murder. On one such raid we lost Ezra the Shoemaker, but heartless Hilda the Harlot mourns him not. "Slow pay and he also made *love* like a shoemaker," spake the tart tartly. Rachel noticed the women of this place working pointed sticks into sheeps' wool to make coverings. "Why, they are knitting Afghans!" she said. Zoomgolli broke a fifty-year silence to shout, "East!" We go east.

Bond snapped his long, tapering fingers. "I'm starting to dig this stuff. Rachel's observation gave us the name Afghanistan."

A series of scrolls Feldspar touched upon in brief told of the dwindling tribe's years in Sinkiang and Mongol-ruled territories. Rachel, now 180, was ailing more frequently. "It has been many a moon since she accorded me the benefits of her womanhood," complained the diarist. Zoomgolli twice cried, "East!" The high priest expired at age 290. Shimon blamed Hilda the Harlot for his death. "She had no right to stimulate a middle-aged man as she would a stripling."

SCROLL TWENTY-EIGHT

The end is near for sweet Rachel. We have traded the last of our pottery for passage across a great sea in the boat of a merchant, Len Ox of Chee Yi Nah, who was so enthralled by it that he proposes to emulate it and name it both in honor of his country and himself. Rachel was leery of the sailship. "Good husband, you do not expect me to ride in that junk, do you?"

Enrapt at the saga, the Dane's audience was playing the game to the hilt. "Hey, she coined the name for the Chinese boat!" said *Detroit News* columnist Doc Greene.

SCROLL TWENTY-NINE

Sweet Rachel breathed her last as our boat touched the shores of this lush paradise whose mountains belch smoke and fire. "May the Lord go with thee, Shimon," she gasped unto me. "It is unfitting for a man to be alone. Press your suit with our last woman, Hilda the Harlot. Purify her in a ritual bath and cleave unto her as a husband." I was inconsolable. Not even Ruben had a decent sooth worth saying. I went to my flesh and blood, weeping, "Zoomgolli, thy mother is dead. Comfort me." Zoomgolli said, "East." I thereupon spake in anger. "My son, hath not the Lord given thee a greater lexicon than the solitary word 'east'?" My son smiled fatuously and spake: "Lexicon." With a sinking heart I perceive we have been led, lo, these many years, by one of unsound mind.

SCROLL THIRTY-ONE

Hilda the Harlot will have none of me, disdaining my proposal in a hateful manner. "I need no doddering fool of two hundred and eighty and his idiot son for a family. My preference is Reuben the Soothsayer. He is two hundred and sixty-five and besides he is a professional man." Zoomgolli brightened and said, "East lexicon." How gratifying to witness his burgeoning intellect! We are the only people on this island, few in number and lonely. Yet we practice our ancient faith, lighting candles on the Sabbath and striving to recall the all but forgotten litanies. Oh, Lord, where hast Thou brought us?

"I have reached the scrolls containing revelations I still find difficult to believe," said Igneous Feldspar.

SCROLL THIRTY-SIX

Hosanna! A boat has crashed upon our shores! From it limped a bedraggled, seasick collection of brownish-yellow, slant-eyed souls from various parts of the great Chee Yi Nah land we traversed, who speak in tongues with which I am conversant. They are pagans who worship crickets and coolie hats. The last of us are endeavoring to teach them our belief in one God Almighty. We have built them an Ark of the Covenant and to hear them repeat the *Sh'ma Israel* gladdens the heart.

Ruben the Soothsayer and Hilda the Harlot were found dead at nightfall. Natural causes.

My loins cry for gratification, yet there is no one to cleave unto. However, one of the newcomers is a maiden, Oshima, fair to behold, whose glances signal the unmistakable message that she, too, wishes cleaving unto. Can such a thing be possible between a man of my hoary years and a maid of fifteen? Under pretext of teaching her to read and write our language I have come close to her often. I shall ask her father for her hand.

SCROLL THIRTY-SEVEN

Consent has been given! How my blood tingles! And Zoomgolli adores her. She cleans out his ears and inserts fresh dead birds every day.

SCROLL THIRTY-EIGHT

We married in the tradition of my faith. Before the ceremony I made her swear to preserve this humble history in a secret place so that in years to come the world may know of the strange destiny that befell one of the lost tribes of Israel.

Our survivors intend to intermarry with the new people as a means of perpetuating our creed. Will we succeed? Or will the pagan ways prevail? Only He knows.

On this last sheet of papyrus I record my thoughts of this promising night. She disrobes before me. I am on fire. It has been decades since Rachel's demise and I feel like a young groom about to taste the bliss of conjugal union for the first time.

"And that," the Dane said, "is the last entry of Shimon."

"*Gevaldt!*" Bond cracked his knuckles. "What a yarn and what a place to break it off! What a shame we'll never know how the old geezer made out."

The others echoed his sentiment, but Feldspar held up his hand. "I said it was the last thing Shimon ever wrote, but on the bottom of the last scrawl is a short passage, obviously jotted by the maiden. It reads: 'Old man clove, fall dead just when Oshima starting to cleave unto. Bad old man. Maybe Zoomgolli better. Oshima want cleaving very fast.'"

"Professor, I apologize." Bouncy blond Regina Tellez of *Look* magazine stood up. "I thought this was going to be one big bomb, but it's turned out to be a bombshell a thousand times bigger than the trawler incident. Oh, how it's going to shake up these islands something fierce!"

"What do you mean?" said the *Cleveland Press*'s James Garrett. "Granted it's a humdinger, great Sunday-supplement stuff, but what's the big deal?"

Feldspar wore a grave, hesitant look. "Miss Tellez' analysis coincides with mine. Can you not see the implications? This very spot, Shimonoshima, is doubtless named in honor of the two principals of that doomed marriage, Shimon, an elder of Israel, and Oshima, who may have come from China, Korea, Malaya or any of the other lands that spawned the Oriental race. Shimon speaks of the 'new people' as pagans worshiping in an animalistic mode before they were taught monotheism by a highly advanced tribe *who were here first*. The conclusion is dramatic: Though the people of Japan at present practice Shintoism, Buddhism, or variants of either, they are the direct descendants of Jews."

Bond fell back howling. "Baron Sanka, as the snake said to Mother Eve, 'How do you like them apples?' Or should I better say—Sank*aleh*?"

The laughing jag died in his throat when Baron Cockamamiyama Sanka stomped off hissing, and Israel Bond realized he had just said something for which, if there had been no one else around, the Number One of the Japanese Secret Service would have killed him.

11
Shell
Shock

"Dr. Yaynu will guide you through the labyrinths, Mr. Bond and Miss Katz," said Igneous Feldspar. "I suffered a leg injury falling over a tent rope last night"—Bond gave the giant a look of gratitude for the lie—"which rules out my participation. My men have left scuba-diving equipment in your tents. I suggest you suit up as a precaution because these cliffs, due to volcanic activity, are filled with cracks into which the sea has rushed. I shall meet you at the entrance to the main cave in ten minutes. And Miss Katz, as a fellow scientist you'll appreciate my concern for the scrolls. Be ever so gentle as you Xerox them."

Sanka, cooled down and chummy again, walked into Bond's tent as he was pulling on his forever amber Lloyd Bridges Seahunt Swimslax and flippers. "More than ever, Izzy-san, it becomes imperative for my government to scrutinize those scrolls. Unfortunately I was unable to convince the news media to withhold the story and thus I fear my people will be psychologically unhinged, their cultural pride shattered. I myself believe the scrolls to be either spurious or, to be charitable, poorly translated. With all due respect to your estimable faith, we Japanese are definitely not Jewish."

Scratch a Manchu and you'll find an anti-Semite, Bond thought. "OK, Cocky-san," was his curt reply. He stopped by for Kopy, helped her strap on her scuba gear and they headed toward the beckoning Dane. The sun flashed off Feldspar's hydrofoil a thousand feet below and Bond had a thought. Was that the craft that would have picked up Aw Gee Minh had he carried out his nefarious scheme?

A Japanese workman, one of a gang of hundreds lugging materiel of all sizes and shapes up the perilous road to the cliff top, slipped in front of him and let a green cylinder clank on its nozzle against a rock. A clear liquid frothed out. "Clumsy fool!" thundered the Dane, an irate flush stealing up to his blond curls. The man cowered as though expecting a blow, but the Dane managed an insincere smile. "Be more careful in the future, my man. The men are bringing up equipage for my Herrosukka Buddha project, Mr. Bond. The Norwegians are progressing at a good pace."

Kopy wrinkled her nose. "Lox."

"And cream cheese to you, luv," Bond riposted.

"No, Iz, I meant—"

Feldspar said quickly, "And here is Dr. Yaynu, your Pied Piper for this excursion. Good morning, Yaynu."

The hawk-faced Bulgarian, wearing a black mock-turtle necked sweater and Levi Strauss jeanlets, nodded a greeting.

"No scuba gear for you, Dr. Yaynu?" Bond said.

Dr. Yaynu's eyes became hooded. "I don't believe I am going as far as you are, Mr. Bond," an averment the Israeli sifted for a double meaning.

The Bulgarian ushered them into blackness and flicked the switch on his outsize flashlight. A monstrous black billepede skittered over the cave floor and Kopy screamed. Dr. Yaynu squashed it indifferently under his half-calf Nancy Sinatras. "Here are many such creatures—scorpions, tarantulas, black widows. Mind where you place your hands."

The passageway slanted downward and they began to smell an overpowering combination of primordial ooze and the musty salt of the sea. Dr. Yaynu's beam picked up myriads of crawlies, each new one sending a spasm through the shapely researcher. Once Bond felt his front foot plunging into a crack and shouted, but Kopy grasped his hand and pulled him free. "Iz, be careful, darling. No telling how deep these things go."

When he heard Kopy gasping for breath, he said, "Let's stop, doctor, and give Miss Katz a rest."

"If you wish, Mr. Bond. Actually we are at the chamber where Skwato found the scrolls of Shimon. We had it widened to accommodate Professor Feldspar. Slide through the opening, Miss Katz, and we shall pass the Xerox to you."

Bond lit a Raleigh. "Go ahead, baby. History awaits you." She smiled, kissed him warmly and knelt at the opening, wriggled through on her tummy and took the Xerox from Bond.

"Iz!" Her voice had a hollow, faraway ring. "They're here! And they're just marvelous!" There was a whirring and clicking and her excited bursts, "Got it! Got it!"

"She will be occupied some time, Mr. Bond. Would you care to see another of the wonders of this place?"

"You're the doctor," said Bond. "Lead on."

They took a left fork and scrambled toward an ever-increasing roar. "An enthralling grotto, Mr. Bond, formed by eruptions and oceanic erosion. It is a sight you'll never forget."

He was not overstating the case. They emerged into a cathedral of nature hewn by ten thousand herculean stonemasons. Below seethed the ocean, this way and that, buffeting the walls with maniacal force.

"Is this not a magnificent place to die, Oy Oy Seven?"

Dr. Yaynu's hand sported a long-barreled Brezhnev-Kosygin.

Israel Bond's lips formed a moue of disgust. "It appears I've let myself be a TUSH pigeon again, Dr. Yaynu—if that's your name."

"It will do for you, Mr. Bond, although it once was General Bolsheeyit, one of the top policymakers of the KGB until you smashed my career by your daring foray into the Soviet Union with matzoh to lighten the hearts of the Russian Jews. It was you who murdered my assassin, Torquemada LaBonza, 'The Man with the Golden Gums.' And it was you who disposed of our bloc's top counterspy, the Bulgarian named Avakum Zakhov, whom we had lent to the Syrians to conduct a campaign of terror under the pseudonym of Feisal Fullah-Sheik." The hawk face hardened into hideous hatred. "Yes, you, Oy Oy Seven, brought me disgrace and forced me to flee Mother Russia, you filthy Zhid!" He smashed the flashlight against Bond's jaw.

Bond said through gritted teeth, "And Holzknicht reached into the grudge file and plucked you out, too, eh, Yaynu? All kinds of ghosts are slithering out of that file, it seems. I suppose you're going to kill the girl as well."

"No, my friend. *Herr Doktor* wishes the world, especially the Japanese, to see the reproductions. I am sure you noted Baron Sanka's dismay at the notion his antecedents were Jewish. Multiply that feeling by one hundred million sons and daughters of Dai Nippon and you will get the picture. Step by step—and there are even greater provocations in the works—they will be irritated into a war against Eretz Israel. I shall tell Miss Katz we went sightseeing and, alas, you slipped on the ledge and fell into the grotto. Move back, Mr. Bond. At the count of three it will be all over."

Bond took a tiny step backward.

"Raz." The ex-KGB bigwig was counting in Russian, an added fillip of revenge for Bond's role in the Matzohball affair. Below, the sea issued a seductive siren's call: *Come on down! You're finished, Oy Oy Seven. Why even wait for the third count? Come on down! Take one more step back and find eternal rest in my bosom.*

His mind telegraphed back: *The hell with you, Tomon the way Dooley, Mrs. Danvers and Rebecca, too! And make that wire collect!*

"Dva." Yaynu ticked off the second count.

But Bond, who'd been measuring the time between counts, was spinning in the graceful pivot taught him by the Big O of the Cincinnati Royals, and at *"Tri"*—three—had his back to the Russian and felt the bullet whang into the heavy-gauge steel of the oxygen tank. He completed the pivot to see Yaynu clutching at the spot in his guts where the slug had ricocheted. Yaynu blatted, but in a final suicidal lunge battered his bullet-like head into Bond's belly.

And they went over.

On the way down Bond was an unstoppable wild man, the crook of his bronze muscular arm crushing his foe's neck, and he screamed a beloved old Passover song into the bluish Slavic face.

"Die, die Yaynu! Die, die, Yaynu! Die, die, Yaynu! Die, Yaynu, die, Yaynu!"

How long they fell he could not be sure—two or three seconds, perhaps—and as he saw the sea rushing to meet him he twisted in midair and swung the body of the strangled Yaynu under him so that it would take the brunt of the impact. Nevertheless his own head exploded in a red network of zigzag pain patterns and he soared to the surface, affixed his face mask, started the oxygen and submerged again, for he'd got the bad news. He was some two hundred feet from the ledge with no way to scale the sheer sides of the grotto. If there was a way out it would have to come from underneath, perhaps a channel to the Pacific. If water had got in, there had to be an egress somewhere. There had to be! He'd only an hour's worth of life-sustaining air; not a pip of a popkin could be wasted.

Round and round Bond swam, examining his watery trap from all sides, his eyes straining to pierce the murky greenness. He tensed. A shadow passed over his head; wicked rows of teeth grinned at him. Barracuda! Ten muscular feet of murder whose

Gillette super-stainless cutting power could serrate him to strips. *Keep swimming at a steady pace,* his heart warned, *or it'll sense your panic and close in. Make believe you're a larger, deadlier fish, a dolphin, say. Nothing dares attack a dolphin.* He sliced toward the bottom and saw a colony of sponges, a bull and several simpering does. Pulling a razor-sharp Solingen-Helm knife from his right flipper, he slashed away at the harem, liberating the great round bull and, bouncing it off his head in the jocular manner of a dolphin at play, made some sportive 'Flipper' noises he hoped would approximate a dolphin's chuckle. It seemed to do the trick. The 'cuda backed off respectfully.

Was that a blessed glimmer of light in the distance? Yes! He gave the bull sponge a friendly farewell pat on its holey buttocks and paddled toward the light, thrilling as he felt the water turning warmer. The light became more intense and his heart leaped. Thank God, he'd found a cut-through to the sea! The current seemed inexorable, but he fought it inch by inch, until he could now see a dimly red ball of fire—the sun! *Stroke, stroke, stroke; you're almost out of here, buddy boy; thirty feet more, twenty, ten....*

The current reversed suddenly. Unbelievably. It was no longer pushing him; it was pulling him. Why?

Gottenu! The suction was damn near wrenching the mask from his face. In a frightening glimpse Bond saw the sun blacked out by something at the end of the tunnel to freedom, something yawning, two valves widening to reveal a pearly ambience. There was a last sucking sound and he was drawn into its midst. The valves snapped shut with sickening finality.

And Israel Bond knew he'd exchanged the frypan for the oven. He was locked inside that most dreaded of all deep-sea denizens, the one-hundred-foot oyster!

12

"When You've Been in the Biggest Oyster There Is"...

A swell tilted the barge sitting in the reef-rimmed Maroon Lagoon—so named because of the trillions of brownish-red microorganisms which stain its waters—sending the brooding American on the camp chair sliding toward his Japanese partner.

"Damn it, Tats, I'm getting sunburned, seasick and fed up with this whole deal, and spare me that patience-of-the-East *shtik*." So spoke Seymour "Sy" Feig, a fortyish, spindly-legged man with thinning brown hair, who wore a raffish Korvette's Acapulcowitz cabana suit—Sy Feig, the fabled, flamboyant press agent who'd discovered Sylvester Soulmeat working on a New York Department of Sanitation truck and in six months made him a rock 'n' roll star. ("Sylvester, baby, if there's one thing I know how to handle, it's *garbage*.") Of late Feig had made his mark as a producer of low-budget, quickie movies—*Born to Flog*, *Leather Whip Beach Party* and *Hell's Angel, Flog Me from Your Dirty Honda*—which were garnering socko grosses at a Forty-second Street theater. The *New York Daily News* critic had given them the highest possible rating—four weals.

Handsome, poised "Tats" Nagashima, the Orient's most prominent show business entrepreneur, tried to mollify his grousing companion. "Sy, we've had a few slow days, true, but you have to admit things have been looking up—literally-all day. A thirty-two-foot crayfish and a forty-one-foot 'pusfeller came out of the lagoon and Clancy got some thrilling footage. Believe me, I wouldn't have asked you to invest your dough and travel more than nine thousand miles if I wasn't sure there were some first-rate, untapped monsters down below. You saw the films I've shot from here—*It Came from the Maroon Lagoon, The Creature from the Maroon Lagoon Versus Frankenstein and the Grandson of the Fly*, etc. Huge moneymakers. It's just a matter of time, that's all."

Feig masticated his unlit Dutchmaster. "Crayfish, octopussys. Passé. You can't pull the public in with crap like that no more. What we need is like a three-hundred-foot dinosaur, the biggest that ever lived—the oedipus rex, wasn't it?—dripping with slime, incensed at impious man, who has disturbed his million-year snooze by detonating a hydrogen bomb, so he comes to the surface to wreak his malice on an unsuspecting world. That's what we need. And what I need personally is that diving chick over there. Geez, what boobs on that broad! Tats, try again, huh? Ask her does she want to be in pictures."

Nagashima yelled something to the almost naked maiden in the little flat-bottomed, high-sided boat, who shook her head in negation. "No dice, Sy."

"Why is she so goddam uppity? What's she got against me?"

"It's a long story. She despises film people. Her name is Go-Down Mikimoto and she is Japan's most beautiful and celebrated pearl diver. Two years ago she was prevailed upon by our film industry to go to the States and play herself in a South Sea epic, *Shark God of Cuticura*. When she was screen-tested they decided she didn't look native' enough, so they gave the part to Raquel Welch. Go-Down suffered terrible indignities at the hands of some lupine movie moguls and swore she would never consort with *gaijins* again. You don't stand a chance."

"Want me to shoot any more calm sea-type exteriors?" said Liam Clancy, the red-faced Irishman in the studiously torn Levi Strauss Sea-Snuggies, who operated the camera and sound.

"Nah." Feig gave the girl a censorious glare.

When it swooshed into the sky Nagashima first assumed it was a waterspout. "Shoot it, Clancy. We'll work it in somewhere."

Then they saw it, the huge white bauble suspended atop the column of water and mist and the two immense blackish valves spread flat at its base. Something hacked and coughed and belched sonorously; there was a long sigh and the valves cracked together and went under.

"Mother of God!" cried Liam Clancy.

"Mother of pearl, you mean," Feig corrected. "That's a pearl, pal, biggest damn one ever. Must be fifty feet around. Hey, it's falling!"

The pearl bounced into the sea, drenching them to the skin in a mountainous spray. Clancy cursed, but stayed at his post filming away in blazing zeal. To pick up the sound of the pearl rolling over the breakers, Clancy boosted the volume and lowered the boom.

Go-Down Mikimoto was a tawny arrow diving from her dory, her supple flanks a symphony of rhythmic precision as she stroked toward the bobbing blob and called to Nagashima.

"This is incredible," said Nagashima. "Go-Down says there's a man inside. We'd better haul it in before it sinks."

"Film, Clancy, film!" With that command, Feig jumped from the barge, Nagashima following closely. They thrashed a foamy path to the girl, whose forefinger was indicating a shadow-figure lurking behind the lustrous covering. The trio, making a monumental effort, pushed the pearl in the direction of the barge, shouting for assistance. Six technicians leaped into the water and together they managed to roll it onto the barge, which rocked menacingly. "Don't tip us. I'm getting shots like you never saw," Clancy cried.

Go-Down banged an impotent fist on the pearl. "Hurry! It must be opened or he will die."

So, you can *speak English, you little cocker,* Feig thought, copping a fast feel that went unnoticed. "You're right, chickie. Hey, you guys, bust this thing apart."

Nagashima and his crew broke up some tables and chairs and used the legs as clubs until there was a sound of splintering, and the pearl split and in a swirl of sand and sea a man fell upon the deck.

Nagashima removed the oxygen tank and face mask.

Feig smacked his hand against his head. *"Gottenu!* Bond! Israel Bond!"

"Sy? Sy Feig, here in Japan?" The gray eyes then focused on the gleaming configuration of Go-Down Mikimoto. "Honey, help me, please. You know the legend of oysters, what they're supposed to do to people? Well, when you've just been inside the biggest oyster there is... Please, baby, please."

Simpatico were the black eyes of Go-Down Mikimoto. "Of course, sir." Wriggling through Feig's fingers, she removed her skimpy loincloth, liberated Bond from the Seahunt suit and snuggled against his chest. An "Ar-r-gh!" savage and primeval, escaped his sensual lips and he seized her with a spasm that shook the barge.

Nagashima hid his eyes considerately. Feig did not.

"Shoot it, Clancy! Shoot it! Damn it, this'll pack em in, by Skouras! Tats, you were one hundred percent right about the Maroon Lagoon. It really came through for us. What a plot!"

Nagashima looked askance at his exuberant confrere. "I concede it's amazing, but what's the plot?"

Feig laughed. "Are you nuts, Tats? A gigantic oyster surfaces, spits out the mother of all pearls; it breaks open to reveal an oversexed Hebraic Hercules who's got to hock a broad or he'll die of frustration; he lands on a gorgeous knish of an Ama diving girl and gives her the hock of ages. That's no plot by you? Hell, Tats, it's"—he strove for a metaphor—"'New Wave'... *avant-goiter!* And we don't screen this one in some *shlock* moviehouse, either. This one goes right to the art theaters."

For the better part of an hour the two splendid anatomies locked and hocked, finding desire's peak in a crystalline explosion. When it was done and the burning deck hosed down by Nagashima's aides, Bond sighed. "Sarah, forgive me. This one was simply uncontrollable."

Feig blinked. Was that a voice? *"Iz, I forgive you, darling."* No, just a keening breeze, he decided.

Bond's eyes were closing now. "Poor bastard oyster. I ruined it, Sy. It'll need a complete valve job...."

His head lolled in Go-Down Mikimoto's lap.

13
The Dane
Talks

"I've been sleeping three days?"

"Yup. Like a top." Feig handed Bond a Schweppes 'n' tonic and watched his buddy down the perky quinine and Jeris. "You look like hell, Iz. Lump on your noggin, shoulder torn up, purple belly bruise. I take it you're still at the old secret-agent business?" When Bond grunted at the indiscretion, he said, "It's OK. Tats here is a close-mouthed type and I don't think this lovely creature, Go-Down Mikimoto, is going to blow your cover, either. Now, how in hell did you get in and out of that Pacific pocketbook?"

Bond lit a Shinsei and gave them a condensed version of his tribulations, beginning with the battle on the JAL jet. "Well, I'd about five minutes of air left and nothing seemed to be working. This may be the wrong adjective, but it was getting *clammy* in there. Oystery sounds better, don't you think? I spent an eternity punching at its meaty interior, then I lifted my face mask and began biting chunks out of it, which explains my shameful deportment, Miss Mikimoto. I'm truly sorry."

"It's Go-Down to you, Mr. Bond, and I'm not." She held another cool slab of shark bladder against his shoulder wound. "An old Ama remedy."

"I'd become resigned to an oystery grave when the principle of how a pearl is formed went through my mind. It's caused by a foreign body that irritates the oyster. Size-wise I was big enough to be a foreign body, yet nothing I did seemed to rile it until I remembered I had the world's most potent irritant in the compartment of my old Captain Midnight decoder ring, a pinch of Mother Margolies' Activated Old World Chrain. I schmeared it smack dab in the middle of the oyster."

"*Chrain* is Yiddish for horse-radish, folks," informed Feig. "Ain't nothin' under the sun got the bite of Mother's *chrain*. It could clear up the sinuses of the chairman of the board of Dristan. Go on, Iz."

"It had been pitch black in there, but after I applied the stuff the meaty mound began to glow. It started to choke and wheeze and then something sticky was enveloping me—nacre, the secretion which, when hardened around a grain of sand, creates the pearl. I felt the nacre solidifying, and then it decided to come up and regurgitate me. I must say, it was a wonderful transition, from nacre to naked. You know the rest. Go-Down, if you hadn't spotted me, I would have smothered inside." Bond suddenly moaned. *Smothered inside.* His fiancée was still in the fetid caves of Shimonoshima, probably dead of suffocation. "Kopy..." The sensual teeth clicked savagely. "If it's the last thing I do, I'll get Holzknicht for that—that is, after I do the screenplay for the sequences you've just filmed." He spent two hours banging away at Feig's Smith-Corona portable. "The usual Screenwriters Guild rates will suffice, Sy, and I'll meet you in New York for the voice dubbing. Now, somebody get me to Shimonoshima, *schnell!*"

"I shall row you there, Mr. Bond," said a desolate Go-Down. "Step into my dory. It is a sturdy craft designed by Horthy of Budapest."

Bond licked his lips in sheer joy. *Gottenu,* what a setup she'd handed him! "A Budapest boat, eh? I guess it's"—his flashing wit laid in one of his most scintillating one-liners—"*hunky dory!*"

As Go-Down Mikimoto churned the oars, her eyes devoured him. So this was Secret Agent Israel Bond, her lover! She had read many novels pertaining to his ruthless breed, the first-rate creations of Le Carré, Deighton, Donald Hamilton, Adam Hall, etc., and enjoyed them all, although she preferred by far the newest writer mining this vein, Sol Weinstein, an exciting, prepossessing American, in whose Pocket Book Specials paperbacks, *Loxfinger, Matzohball* and *On the Secret Service of His Majesty, the Queen* ($1 per copy; mail orders filled promptly, gratefully by Pocket Books, Inc., 630 Fifth Avenue, New York, N.Y.; no extra charge for author's autograph or body), she'd found an approach to sex and violence unexplored by the others. How cruelly handsome Mr. Bond was! He reminded her of photographs she had once seen of the young George Gershwin.

At the landing in Shimonoshima, Go-Down faced him for what might be the last time. "Shall I ever see you again, Mr. Bond?"

"Our fates will lead us to one another again, Go-Down. In the meantime, love me...Never, never change... Keep that breathless charm... Don't you rearrange it ... 'Cause I love you ... etc., I want to think of you as I saw you first, a proud untamed mermaid. I would recommend two minor alterations—Westernizing your eyes and lightening your pigmentation by drugs—but otherwise stay as you are." He kissed her passionately and stepped onto the shore.

"And I shall be ever afloat near this village should you require me," the Ama nymph said, but her pledge never reached his ears, for Bond was clambering up the path to the tent city, bowling over sweating Japanese bearing more paraphernalia on their backs, and in ten minutes he'd gained the top. He stopped in his tracks, shivering.

The Great Herrosukka Buddha regarded him from suspicious slitted eyes.

Gottenu! They'd built it up to its hundred-foot height in seventy-two hours. Palpably the Great Dane and his Norwegians were geniuses at this trade. Bond walked to the base, feeling somehow that the eyes were following his every step. At the feet he came upon a pile of bleached bones, which he nudged with his foot.

"Please do not disturb them, Mr. Bond. These are some of the remnants of bygone worshipers and their donkeys who died at the Buddha's feet after the torturous climb. I have left them as a memorial to all those who have genuflected here."

From the shadow of the Buddha stepped Professor Igneous Feldspar.

"I knew in my heart you possessed the leonine courage to survive, Mr. Bond." The giant sounded genuinely relieved. "You are destined for greater glories."

Bond lit a Raleigh. "Prof, we've got some palavering to do. Whether you know it or not, I have been threatened from the moment I neared this land by an undercover neo-Nazi organization known as TUSH." He unfolded the narrative. "I am of the opinion that Holzknicht has a hold on you. Magma told me of your apprehension for 'the boy' in a little" —he found himself blushing—"chat we had one night. Come clean, Feldspar, and I'll do my best to extricate you from his clutches."

The Dane expelled the sigh of a man who has been carrying a secret onus too long. "Yes, Ernst has a hold on me. In the late 1920's we were fellow students at the Schisselzelmknist Institute of Psychiatry and Medicine in Berlin. Even then Ernst Holzknicht was astounding his professors with concepts beyond their understanding. He was first to cure a moribund loaf of bread by massive injections of penicillin, the first to train a dog to shout at the clang of an alarm: 'Meat-bell! Meat-bell!' Ernst was a misanthrope, who despised his brother students and instructors. For some odd reason he was drawn to me; why, I cannot say—my Danish jollity or my outlandish size, perhaps. Whatever the reason, we became firm friends, although we had many a heated polemic over the ascendant Nazi philosophy which had begun to infect him. I well remember the day he told me flatly, 'The world will never be a decent place until I destroy all the Jews.'"

"I recall a similar dialogue with the good *Herr Doktor* in the cellar of a gambling casino. Pray, continue."

"Graduation parted us, although we corresponded for many years until the day the *Boche* swarmed into Denmark. I had no further wish to fraternize with a man who was using his God-given genius to further the cause of maniacs. Besides, I had married a charming Oslo poetess some years before and was immersed in the bliss of family life. Her name was Helvig Rolvig, winner of the Nobel Prize for her only published collection of poetry, a 350-page, two-couplet volume, *Reflections from the Middle Ear*. She was a great one for copious footnotes."

"Helvig Rolvig was *your* wife?" Bond's eyes softened and he recited the well-remembered lines:

> Apes and grapes
> Have dissimilar shapes.

"I've adored her poems since I was a gawking teener. How happy you must have been."

"Ah, under that hard-boiled, cruelly handsome facade is the soul of a dreamer, Mr. Bond. Yes, we were sublimely happy. But the very spirit of independence that flavored her poetry cost her her life. A Nazi officer who also admired her works commanded her to either compose a poem in his honor or die by firing squad. I shall never forget the way she drew herself up and cried:

For you?
Oh, pooh!

and her horror when she realized that in her defiance she'd done what she'd sworn not to do—compose a poem. She snatched a rifle from a guard's hands and killed herself on the spot."

"How awful."

"Luckily there is a living reminder of Helvig Rolvig, our only child, Knute, whom I raised myself. He grew to be a strapping lad and is something of a scientist himself. His specialty is graffitology, the discovery and translation of graffiti, those pithy wall scrawlings. Spelunking in the Swiss Alps, Knute discovered graffiti most certainly chipped into cave walls by early man, among them: 'Would you want your daughter to marry a Lake Dweller?' and 'The fool seeks fire from flintstones; the hippie uses a Zippo.' By this time Knute no longer needed me, Mr. Bond, and I was a lonely man craving companionship, but unable to give a woman pleasure because of a rare penile affliction that strikes old men—a monk's hood. On an aimless jaunt into Copenhagen's night life I met, wooed and eventually won the present Mrs. Feldspar. Do not be embarrassed, my friend. I am aware of her sexual need for you. To resume, we honeymooned in Berlin, where out of the blue I received a call from Ernst—after all those years of estrangement. I prayed he would be regenerate, but he wasted no time informing me he had kidnapped Knute and would kill him unless I became involved in a charade to be played out in Japan. I now see that Skwato and the man who called himself Dr. Yaynu were his minions. You probably have guessed that Dr. Yaynu killed the fisherman Nikko Tee-Yin. And it was my hydrofoil that was to fetch Aw Gee Minh from the Pacific. How happy I was when I realized he had failed. You showed great resourcefulness as usual, Mr. Bond."

"What about the scrolls?"

"They are genuine. They must be. How can I, who am so knowledgeable in this field, be mistaken?"

"Real or false, they cost a sweet kid her life. Kopy Katz."

"Oh, but she is alive."

Bond's knees buckled and he braced himself against a toe of the Buddha. "Alive?"

"When all of you were gone so long I sensed tragedy and despite my gammy leg I led a search party into the caves. We found her unconscious on the blood-spattered ledge where you and Dr. Yaynu had your difference of opinion. She had heard the shooting and rushed to your aid. She thought you had died. Baron Sanka has taken the poor child back to Tokyo."

"I want Holzknicht. Is he in Japan?"

"I—I cannot—"

"You've got to help me nail him, professor. I know what your son means to you. Israel's millions mean as much to me. If Holzknicht isn't brought to heel, unimaginable devastation is in the offing for two countries."

Igneous Feldspar looked into the insistent gray eyes. "You are right. I shall cooperate. Ernst has told me to register at the New Fujiya Hotel in Atami, where I am to receive further instructions. I shall transport you to Honshu in my hydrofoil on the morrow."

"Good Dane, Great Dane," Bond said. "If I had a can of Red Heart I'd feed it to you right now. You've earned it. But I'll do something better. I'll save you, your son and Japan and Israel."

"And save me before I go mad, for heaven's sake!" The voice, hoarse and demanding, came out of a thickly blossomed *yoni* bush. Something flew at his ankles and pinned him against the rocks. It was Magma Feldspar, naked and on fire. "Iggie, you no-score *klutz;* beat it while I make it with the King of Swing!"

"Professor, I—"

"Do as she asks, Mr. Bond. I understand." The golden curls drooped over the hurt eyes and he shuffled away on his Frankenstein-monster walk.

"There's nothing I won't do for a friend," Bond yelled to the giant, but Magma's lips, voracious and vampirish, crushed his words back into his sensual tonsils. "Screw thee and thy goddam goodness, lover boy. Let's make it."

"Up thine, baby," Bond riposted.

They made it.

Sarah cried.

No one listened.

14
A Fitting Climax
Requires a Fitting

The Great Herrosukka Buddha blinked an indifferent farewell to the hydrofoil swerving around the cliff. "One positive thing has come from this deviltry," said the Dane. "The Buddha is rebuilt. My Norwegians will stay behind to coat its fiber glass body with a bronze spray. Hopefully, when you've brought this evil affair to a successful conclusion, I shall rejoin them in a few days to make a final inspection. By the next festival it will be ready to receive worshipers."

"Fiber glass. That's how you people got it up so fast."

"Bronze, my friend, is too expensive and too heavy. It would have taken years to haul a thousand tons up those cliffs and sculpt it. Ibsen's fiber glass bulk was easily transportable and malleable, and it is resilient enough to withstand any climatic conditions."

Feldspar had scheduled a conference on the scrolls at Meiji University, but he promised to meet Bond in two days at the Atami hotel. "I'll be there, too, Gray Eyes," chimed in Magma.

The hydrofoil made its elegant way past freighters and launches and put in at Pier 12, and Bond and the Dane shook hands. "Until then," said the latter, assaying a graceful leap back onto the deck, but the giraffe legs failed him and he tumbled into a cluster of his crew.

Those damn legs, Bond thought. Poor bastard has no coordination at all. What hell it must be to forever totter like a wino in a world of surefooted men.

Ginza-Burg, whom he'd phoned from Kyushu, was waiting in the Cedric. "As you requested, Oy Oy Seven, I didn't tell the Baron. It's gonna be a real surprise. We'd all given you up for lost. Maybe you can do something about these," and he dumped three English editions of local newspapers in Bond's lap.

In a front-page editorial the *Japan Times* expressed rancor at "the piratical attack" by the trawler and the contents of the scrolls. "These alleged historical documents, of which we have seen only Xerox copies, threaten the very soul of the islands. Can they be another Israeli machination?" The Yomiuri paper called for "suspension of relations with the Mideast aggressor. One can now appreciate the belligerence of the Arab states if this is what they have had to contend with since 1948." Signed by "Parker Waterman," the Asahi editorial went a step further: "A proud people must unsheath its sword, if need be, to keep from being sullied by Zionist marauders and doctrines."

Ginza-Burg, executing a slick Fangio sideswerve, forced a crowded bus into a ravine. "Gotcha, you cockers! All six dozen! That Asahi piece worries me, Mr. Bond. As you might suspect, Parker Waterman is a pen name. He's Britt Kato, the Minister of Propaganda, and you can take what he wrote as the official line. The Nips are getting a little *fahrbrent*."[*]

Bond consumed seventy-six Raleighs and, when he ran out, three coupons, finding no noticeable difference. Bad business, this mounting Japanese truculence. *Herr Doktor* had once again correctly read the mentality of a nation. Under the servility, smiles and politesse skulked the old samurai war spirit, longing to be unleashed. One couldn't blame Feldspar for that martial characteristic or for the scrolls' revelations. But Shimon's scribblings, compounded with whatever new insults Holzknicht was planning, were bound to cause big trouble. The Nazi had to be liquidated before the lid blew off.

Bond had planned a grand entrance cum trumpet fanfare, but he whipped the Selmer from his lips when he heard the desperate voice of Kopy Katz in the Baron's Cathouse of the August Tea suite.

"No, Baron. Please. It's not your fault."

"I have dishonored myself, Miss Katz. Mr. Bond was my guest, his personal safety my obligation, yet I allowed him to die. Only *seppuku* can cleanse my sin. A simple slash from my right eyeball to my pancreas—"

"No, Cocky!" Bond bashed his way through the paper screen to come upon the tableau he'd expected: Sanka in a black kimono,

---

[*]   Burned up

the sword held high to pierce the stocky body; a cringing, power-less Kopy. "Give me that sword, you damn fool!"

The command triggered off Sanka, who went into a posture of offensive swordsmanship and swiped at Bond, the blade leaving a long, bright gash in the Selmer's mouth.

"Iz!" Kopy fainted over the low table.

"Mr. Bond, as you being away Ipanema making berry, berry many packets of thousand-yen notes. Take them prease."

"Not now," Bond growled, but in shoving away the geisha tugging his arm he let himself be exposed to a second swipe, which drew a thin red line across his knuckles. He sidestepped a third, aimed a half-strength Oyama *bari* kick. Good-o! The tip of his Tijuana Brass bedsock mashed the stubby brown finger on the sword handle and the weapon clattered on the tatami. Sanka, his eyes rolling and maddened, chopped a calloused knuckle into the stomach bruise left by Yaynu's bullet head, which would have killed an ordinary man not possessing the steel-banded muscles Bond had toughened by one thousand pushups between his right-wing Minuteman orange juice and Wheat Chex with Alba nonfat milk each morning. The Israeli saw an opening, brought the Selmer down on the Baron's head. There was a cavernous *klonk* and Sanka fell unconscious over the inert Kopy.

"Dizzy never swung a Selmer like that," Bond said to no one in particular and when no one answered was not disappointed. He slapped Sanka's cheeks sharply and the *Kyodo Kikaku* chieftain came to, fully recovered from his derangement.

"I cannot believe my eyes, Izzy-san. You have returned from the dead. But only *seppuku* can atone for my shame lest the gods be—"

"I'm hip to this bag by now," Bond cut in. "Call in Flowering Fungus." Sanka did and the geisha scurried to his side. "Cocky, tell her to sing that ballad of Raykko once more."

Her first toneless note in the basso profundo convinced him. "Baron, I'd hoped her singing would have improved enough to warrant sparing her life. It hasn't. Let it be her."

Sanka agreed and tossed the geisha the sword. She bowed low and left the suite.

"*Yo-i!*" Bond said. "Now your deities and my muse have been placated." He splashed sake in Kopy's oval face to revive her and detailed his adventure since the cave episode, omitting the Go-Down Mikimoto interlude for the sake of her susceptibilities.

"The 'Black Room,'" she murmured. "It's got to be the 'Black Room.'"

"This is no time for gibberish, baby," Bond said impatiently. "Holzknicht is due in Atami and I've got to get to the top tailor in town on the double."

"A tailor? I do not understand, my friend."

"Baron, it is unthinkable for me to have it out with him in these rags. When you're heading toward the climax of your career as the world's *ichi-ban* secret agent you need groovy threads."

Once he saw the gravity of the situation, Sanka did not hesitate to recommend Ling Ah Lingle, a Chinese Jew from Hong Kong, whose sign in the basement of the grand old prestige hotel, the Imperial, advertised: SUITINGS FOR SPIES, IF YOU'VE GOT THE DAGGER, I'VE GOT A CLOAK TO MATCH IT.

In the window were some end-of-season specials Kopy thought darling. "Iz, I love those silken rope sandals."

"They can be unraveled by pulling on a couple of hidden knots, which gives you a reliable pair of Calcutta strangling cords. In the trade we call sandals like those 'Thug Boats.' That shorty nightie is for KGB girls; the big puffy buttons have death pills inside. Hey, that's a helluva nice Harry Palmer slip-on heat-seeking sweater. Changes from dull brown to bright orange in the presence of a passionate enemy female agent. Mr. Ling Ah Lingle has a pretty spiffy line."

The paunchy proprietor listened attentively to Bond's sartorial needs. "None of the items in my regular stock are for you, sir. They would be appropriate if you were going up against SMERSH, Phoenix, the Gehlen group or the Wackenhut Organization, not TUSH. You require what I would term 'confrontation clothing.'"

"That's the ticket." Chap knew his business. "And the finest bedsocks money can buy. The whole wardrobe can be put on the account of Eretz Israel."

"Eretz Israel? Bedsocks?" The man's butterball face split into a smile of homage. "There is but one man in 'the game' who attaches such importance to bedsocks, who slithers in the dark jungle of espionage for the Star of David. You are Israel Bond, Oy Oy Seven. This is the privilege of a lifetime, Mr. Bond. I shall outdo myself." Humming and measuring, stopping to comment how pleasurable it was to clothe such a physique, Ling Ah Lingle hit a new high in haute couture. The stunning ensemble started with Penkiovsky Paper Pantaloons, a Baby Jane Holzer minidicky, a breathtaking Georgy Girl cummerbund, a pure silk black-and-tan Gypo Nolan trenchcoat (it cost twenty pounds), and he capped it by slipping onto Bond's sensual feet a pair of virtually unobtainable Abominable Snowman bedsocks, each one three feet long, which he swore had been chipped from the feet of an actual Yetta—a female Yeti—discovered in 1921 under a Valley of the Blue Moon snowslide.

There was a moment of uncertainty at the full-length mirror; but then Bond preened and saw himself as an effulgent rainbow, each item a perfect complement to the others, and the joyous tears washed his darkly handsome cheeks.

"Oh, Lord, it's so—so—kicky! Dr. Ernst Holzknicht, you will meet your doom at the hands of the most madly Mod, switched-on spy the world has e'er beheld."

Ling Ah Lingle was still dancing when the little old lady in the blue-and-white shawl entered his shop.

"Ach, did I not see Israel Bond as I passed the Japan Travel Bureau at the other end of the arcade? He departed so rapidly I had no chance of catching him on these old legs."

"He was here, madam, but he's left for the Hilton. He—" and the Chinese stopped abruptly. He'd no business revealing the comings and goings of his clientele. "I must ask you to forget my indiscretion, madam."

"Oh, he'll want to see me, I know. *Shalom,* Ling Ah Lingle." She gave him an engaging smile and returned to the arcade.

The haberdasher lifted the receiver of his telephone. "Operator, please connect me with the message desk at the Hilton."

He had an afterthought and replaced the phone in its cradle. *She said,* "Shalom," he thought. An old lady in a blue-and-white shawl, the colors of Eretz Israel, who uses *Shalom* as her valediction...

He barked a relieved laugh and went about his business.

15
Brolly Brawl On The Bullet

The first caller was Sanka. "Izzy-san, you have forty-eight hours to clear up this affair. If you do not, I cannot be responsible for my government's actions. I have just spent a most unpleasant hour in the Diet office of Propaganda Minister Kato. He showed me a disgusting collection of hate telegrams that has been pouring in from all over the globe since those accursed scrolls were promulgated. Some of the salutations include: 'Emperor Hirosheeny,' 'Hiro-Kike-O,' 'Honorable Number One Mockyo of Tokyo'—those are the milder ones. You cannot expect Japan to put up with further affronts. I shall meet you on the train to Atami." He added a frigid *"Ohayo"*[*] and hung up.

"Wisconsin to you," Bond raged at the dial tone.

A woman from the Tokyo Jewish Center was the second caller. "We have heard you are a public relations spokesman for Mother Margolies' Activated Old World Products. Are you still available for talks before women's groups?"

The anger oozed out of him. "Yes, my dear. I'm leaving for Atami on the 3 P.M. *Bullet*, but buzz me in a day or two. I'll be delighted to address your sisterhood."

He packed his new wardrobe, slipped into some informal attire—robin's-egg-blue Fruit of the Loom Underwonders, rose-colored Don Loper mini-Bimini shorts and cigar-brown Erik Is Here bedsocks with Viking prows on the toes—and buzzed Ginza-Burg, who gunned the Cedric toward Tokyo Central Station at his usual clip, eight dead pedestrians per block. "You'd better get in all the killing you can, *boychikl*," Bond said, "because we Hebes might not be welcome around these parts much longer. Second thought, let *me* take the wheel," which he did at

---

[*]   Good morning

the next stoplight. Slamming the pedal to the floor, he waffled three policemen and twenty-one shoppers.

Boarding the *Bullet* with Sanka, who was nattily dressed in Ainu bearskin leotards, Bond was beset by uneasiness. Just what would Japan do if he couldn't squash TUSH? Launch a war against Eretz Israel? Surely a piddling attack at sea and a few pieces of racist literature wouldn't justify that drastic a response. The Nips might break off diplomatic relations, but that would be tolerable. Then again, they might begin supplying to the Arabs the cream of their technology; that wouldn't be. How sticky it got depended on the next demon from Holzknicht's Pandora's box. Damn it, here he was going into mortal combat with the archenemy minus a single major-league espionage device from Lavi HaLavi. Why had Lavi flipped his dandruff when he needed the little QM's brainpower so urgently?

His melancholia was interrupted by a genteel knock on his compartment door. "Mr. Bond?" One of those adorable little train girls who sell sandwiches and soft drinks smiled shyly at him. "A Western woman requires your presence in Compartment 13."

"What does she look like?"

"Very ancient, sir, and wearing a shawr. She said a strange phrase to me—'*Sharom Areichem.*' This way, prease."

"*Gottenu!* What the hell is M. doing in Japan to complicate things just as this caper is moving toward a finale? Cocky, you'll pardon me for a mo'."

At Compartment 13 he used the present month's simple door signal, pounding out a Chico Hamilton 12/9 cadence left-handed, a Mongo Santamaria bongo riff right-handed, and whistling from both sides of his mouth simultaneously the two themes from Jobim's "No More Blues."

The door slid open.

Her back was to him, but he could see the babushka atop her silver-blue Larry Mathews senior-bopper wig and the blue-and-white shawl, and the love he bore her flooded away the angry speech he'd been rehearsing.

She turned. A venomous, lined face glared at him, the metal tip of a black umbrella dug viciously into his belly bruise. "Hands behind the neck. Walk in slowly. Use your shoulder blades to slide the door shut."

Buddy boy, you deserve anything you're going to get in this four-by-four death trap, he castigated himself. *Is M. the only shawl-draped old Western woman in the world?*

One whiff of her *parfum*, "Forever Eichmann," told him all he needed to know.

"So, you are the *Jude* who killed my son."

The metal tip prodded him twice more, but he dared not retaliate. This was an all too familiar bit of weaponry. It could protect you from the rain, yes, and also spread your intestines apart with an expanding dumdum bullet. You could call it either a "brolly-blaster" or a "bumbershooter," because of the Luger built into the harmless-looking umbrella, without which a conservative Londoner would seem naked.

"There must be some mistake, madam. I am a public relations—"

"You are Israel Bond, the *schweinhund* who killed my only son. I am Frau Ilse Marlene."

Marlene! Of course, the mother of Willi Marlene, the knife-toting member of TUSH's elite branch for killer homos, the Gayfia, whose windpipe Bond had stove in during a hectic incident at London's Gayboy Club in the Queen adventure. "Madam, I—"

Blim! Blam! Her left hand smote his own windpipe. "I believe that is how you did it, *nein?*" *Splish! Splash!* Two more chops split his sensual lips and he retched on the blood pouring into his swollen throat.

"I am afraid you will be in no condition to deliver that speech at the Tokyo Jewish Center, Herr Bond. Yes, it was I who called. Like my late son, I have had theatrical training."

Grand Guignol, no doubt, Bond thought.

"How simple it was to deceive you and your tailor. A simple Hebrew phrase, a few stage props—babushka, shawl, wig—and you let your minds see what you wanted to see—your beloved M."

"The grudge file, Frau Marlene?"

"*Ja.* But I will tell you, since it will not matter in any case, that I am disobeying orders. I was ordered to tag you, but I shall not be robbed of the chance to end your derring-do for all time, Herr Bond."

"One question, *bitte,* Frau Marlene." If her answer was negative, a bobby-pin-size chance remained. "Have you ever ridden the *Bullet* before?"

A tinge of respect entered the toad face. The Jew was not going to whine for his life. "*Nein,* this is my first trip on a *Japanischer* train."

Bonds left hand edged behind him, found a steel clothes hook on the door and clamped around it with all his power. "I presume, Frau Marlene, that brolly-blaster is the same weapon that took the life of—oh, what was his name?" He assumed a quizzical expression. *Stall, stall, Oy Oy Seven!* "Colonel Onan Lemming of the British M.I. 5 in the Liverpool Airport slaying of 1964...."

The *Bullet's* screech was Mozart to his ears.

He'd been braced for the sudden stop, but the unaware hag flew across the compartment and her head caroming off the steel wall was the sweet sound of Mike Epstein's forty-ounce Louisville Schlooger kissing a fast ball into the right-field bleachers. Bond sprang onto the dazed woman, chopping down on her right wrist, and the brolly-blaster fell onto the seat. Infuriated at the startling turnabout, Frau Marlene shook her head to clear away the cobwebs and then snaked back at him, her bony claws raking his cheeks. Her left hand darted to an exposed stocking top and freed a length of silver. But before her hand could complete the deadly arc, Bond had the brolly-blaster pointed dead center at her maddened face, depressed the trigger and—*splat!* Frau Marlene had an extra mouth where her wartstippled nose had been. There was a blood-choked wail; the dirk fell from the wizened fingers and she collapsed on the floor into a bundle of old rags.

Hearing a hammering at the door, Bond wiped the blood from his lips with the back of his hand and opened it to meet the sharp scrutiny of Sanka.

The Baron examined the garbage heap that had been Frau Ilse Marlene without comment.

"Your statement came back to me when I was under the gun, Cocky. 'Some three million people per annum choose the railroads as their method of self-destruction.' One of them paid off for me. Who was it?"

Sanka smiled sardonically. "I have just seen the mangled body on the tracks, Izzy-san, with the note pinned to its kimono. Your savior was Suicide Suzuki."

16
Bowling Brawl in the Bathhouse

"Yes," said Sanka, reflecting upon the event as the cab neared the New Fujiya, "you escaped death at the Nazi woman's hands because of a magnificent act by our eminent chronicler of death. Suicide Suzuki, as it turns out, lived in a luxurious villa on a hill overlooking the New Tokkaido rail bed. His note stated that his last column contained a typographical error that resulted in the misspelling of one of the suicide's names. Instead of haranguing the printer, as he would have been well within his rights to do, he shouldered the blame squarely, apologized to the publisher and the victim's family, went to his home, donned a ceremonial kimono, took out several scrapbooks containing all the "Death Beat" columns he'd ever written, ate them in penance, rupturing his insides, then climbed to the top of his villa and hurled himself onto the tracks. A glorious way to leave this vale of tears, Izzy-san. The gods are smiling now."

Atami, oft referred to as Japan's Coney island by people who have been to neither, nestles, nestles by the Pacific behind a high seawall. On the tiny beach are piles of boulders cut into the shape of monstrous children's jacks. In the rear of the resort are bluffs and mountains from whose terraced ridges hang hotels, both Western and *ryokan*. Its narrow streets bustle with kimono-wearing Japanese on holiday, their omnipresent cameras clicking away in the national sport, the taking of pictures of other Japanese taking pictures.

The resort's newest sensation is the waterfront nightclub-restaurant, the Psyche-Deli, where the country's growing number of English-speaking acidheads congregates to eat delicatessen and dig an incongruous combination of hip American entertainment and those leave-nothing-to-the-imagination Japanese "strip shows." For an additional fee slipped surreptitiously to the crafty-eyed proprietor, Tripleader Taramuki, they will find minute cubes of LSD hidden in the greasy hearts of pastrami sandwiches.

Bond and Sanka joined the Feldspars at a ringside table. "You will enjoy the Psyche-Deli, Izzy-san," said Sanka. "Here performs Japan's *ichi-ban* stripper, Pickup Pochiko, whose control of her—ah—private region is so masterful that she is able to pick up a hundred-yen note without using her fingers or toes."

"We have one in Herzlia who can do that and also make change," Bond said. *There, Cocky-san, a little Israeli chauvinism for you!*

The secret agent, his "confrontation" clothes augmented by a shoulder holster which cuddled to its leathery bosom a five-shot Stitt-Coltrane, searched the Great Dane's face for the recognition signal that would say: *Let us make an excuse to leave the others, Mr. Bond. We have an appointment.*

Feldspar's smile said: *Not yet.*

In the wake of the stripper followed expatriate American jazzman Cassius Clink, inventor of the vibraskull, the controversial instrument that had caused him to be banned from his homeland. Clink, ranked by critics with Gillespie, Parker and Tristano as a primogenitor of the modern school, had by accident found his bag during a brawl in a San Francisco bistro, *The Starving W.* Wielding a bottle of Jack Daniels in self-defense, he discovered that human skulls had a vast spectrum of sounds—alto, tenor, soprano, bass, baritone, etc. By arranging selected individuals into a battery of "living tones" and perching himself on a stool high above them and swinging six-foot mallets, he'd created the vibraskull.

He was scheduled for a thirty-minute set but had to end it at five when in the middle of a driving, double-time passage on "You Go to My Head" three of his "living tones" ceased to be that way. "This," said a disappointed Bond, "is the inevitable result of a Cassius Clink concert. But he still deserves the unstinting adulation of the jazz world. He is the father of the head arrangement."

Two porters mopped up the grisly leavings of the aborted session and then over the loudspeaker came the cry: "Limbo! Let's do de limbo, mon!" Cheering wildly, the Psyche-Deli patrons thronged the floor for the limbo contest, the traditional highlight of the evening in any Japanese nightery from Tokyo's swanky New Latin Quarter to those dingy taverns for the *eta*, the country's "untouchable" class. Bond noted the childish docility of the patrons being led under the ever-lowered limbo stick until it was scant inches from the floor. The hands-down winner was a Tokyo University student, who accepted the trophy from his position under the rug.

The room went black; strobe lights began to wink, and so did Feldspar, slowly and deliberately, three times. Sanka saw Bond and the Dane locked in a conspiratorial glance and remarked, "Good hunting, gentlemen."

Twice on the ten-minute ride up a mountain trail the cab driver had to stop. "There is a bad knock in the motor." He could not locate the source despite a diligent investigation.

"There is nothing wrong with the motor," the Dane said. "Please drive on." His wise eyes messaged Bond: *Control yourself, my friend. Your heart is beating like a Maytag washer.* Bond sucked in a few deep breaths and his heartbeat reverted to its normal 565 counts per minute.

The journey ended in front of a building positioned precariously on a pine-tree-covered cliff. "This is the Samarra Bathhouse, Mr. Bond. I have been instructed to be on the roof garden at midnight. We have a few minutes. Let us use them in a refreshing *ofuro*."

Samarra. Bond's cruel, sensual mouth was framed in an ironic smile. What a fitting place for an appointment!

Feldspar handed a sullen cashier a ten-thousand-yen note and they were shown by lovely maidens in gym uniforms to separate cubicles. Bond disrobed and splashed about in the tub, declining his masseuse's offer of a three-thousand-yen "speciar massage."

"I believe that autoeroticism is a matter for the individual and, besides, it should only be practiced in Cadillacs, young woman."

He dressed quickly, rechecked his Stitt-Coltrane and rapped on the door to Feldspar's cubicle. "Four minutes, professor."

The Dane wore a light-blue *yukata* and as he tottered up the stairs on his giraffe legs Bond noticed his knees were circled by bands of thick grayish scar tissue. Feldspar must have had some horrible car accident, he thought. No wonder the man had no control over his gait.

At eleven-fifty-seven they were on the third floor, Feldspar sliding open a screen, and then on the roof garden. The ocean's scent was pervasive and heavy here. Hundreds of feet below, whitecaps rolled in to end their existence against the boulders and seawall.

"Ouch!" The Israeli shattered the silence by banging his toe into an unyielding mass. Flicking on his Zippo, he saw a pyramid of big black iron balls. "What the hell are they?"

"Souvenirs of the Russo-Japanese War of 1905, Mr. Bond. They are cannonballs used to sink Czarist ships in the battle of Tsushima Strait. After the war they were recovered by the thousands by Imperial divers and brought to Japan, where they are venerated as symbols of national might. It is a poor bathhouse, indeed, that does not have a similar pyramid on its premises."

"It's eleven-fifty-nine. You sure he's going to show?"

"Ernst has the Germanic obsession with punctuality. He will announce his presence at the stroke of midnight; no earlier, no later."

Bond was on a countdown, his heart doing mad flip-flops, ping-ponging off his kidneys, gall bladder and liver. Thirty-three seconds, thirty-two, thirty-one... Surely there should have been a noise on the stairs by now.

The second and hour hands embraced at twelve.

A blinding light flared at the far end of the roof garden. Under a floodlight, sitting in a wheelchair, was a man in a white lab coat, his black hair trimmed in a military crewcut.

Dr. Ernst Holzknicht.

He was not alone. Kneeling by his side and cocking a Manchester-Schlesinger rifle was a tough-looking, slant-eyed mulatto, heavily lipsticked and rouged, his wiry figure encased in a coral Pucci blouse and Braniff Airlines hostess skirt. High-heel Kitty Kelly light-opera pumps of patent leather gleamed in the floodlight. Bond knew the breed—a member of the notorious Black Dragqueen Society, the Far Eastern cult of deviate slay-for-payers. From the mulatto's obscenely curved lips dangled a long yellow cigarette exuding a sweet, acrid tang. A king-sized Chiquita Bananajuana! Just the sort of cigarette to inflame the high yellow into a yellow high—for murder!

The smirking voice that had plagued Bond in a million nightmares spoke. "Listen and do not interrupt." The mouth moved in an odd, jerky way; so did the hands. "So, Oy Oy Seven, you have come to Japan to exact revenge and quash my operation here. Too long have you been a thorn in the side of neo-Nazism. You and your Secret Service are responsible for the deaths of Lazarus Loxfinger, our god; East German Secret Agent James Bund; Gerda 'Auntie' Sem-Heidt, and a host of other TUSH patriots. Your daring feat atop the Empire State Building put me in this wheelchair with a broken body. You have induced this grotesque pig of a Dane to betray me. But you made a foolhardy move by coming here tonight. You will never leave here alive. As for you, Feldspar, you will rue the day you cast your lot with this *Jude*. I shall permit you to live long enough to see your beloved son injected with my new *barbarella* toxin. Shall I describe its unimaginable agony to you, the rotting of tissue—"

"Boche! Boche!" the Dane screamed and broke into his laughable gait toward the Nazi, his hands knotted into fists, the golden curls jiggling.

"Stop him!" Holzknicht commanded.

The Black Dragqueen's rifle buzzed and Feldspar seemed to hang suspended for a second as one of the slugs thudded into his leg, but his rage was as towering as his size and he lunged onward like a crazed bull. Bond's Stitt-Coltrane was out, crashing its entire clip at the Black Dragqueen, but the five bullets missed by a wide margin, blowing out a section of the railing behind the Nazi and his gunsel.

From the Manchester-Schlesinger came an unerring response; there was a searing jolt in his gun hand and the Stitt-Coltrane went flying over the roof. *Thwack!* Another M-S slug hit Bond's right thigh with a tremendous impact, driving him into the pyramid of cannonballs.

Feldspar's hands were inches away from throttling the Nazi's throat when the giraffe legs could take it no longer. He sprawled at the foot of the wheelchair, sobbing impotent curses.

Israel Bond had already made up his mind what his do-or-die tactic would be the instant his head cracked into the top ball. He summoned up his last ounce of power, hoisted the ball and went into the old Don Carter four-step the kegling ace had taught him one night at the White Horse Bowling Academy in Trenton, New Jersey. Now he was on the fourth step of the approach, then his rippling back and shoulder muscles released the cannonball in a mighty thrust.

The Black Dragqueen tittered at the puny effort, but then he froze in horrified fascination, unable to pull the trigger, as he saw the ball gaining momentum and coming at him on a thunderous roll. Before he could snap out of his panic, it was too late. The ball crunched into his ankle, hurling him on a side slant into the bottom of Holzknicht's wheelchair, and suddenly both of them were falling back through the gaping hole in the railing, down, down, down... and the screams of the Black Dragqueen were lost in the pounding of the whitecaps.

Bond forced his bloodied frame to crawl inch by inch to the edge and gazed down at the precise moment the moon scudded out from behind a cloud to bathe the seawall in silvery light. There was the wheelchair in a thousand fragments on the boulders... a white-sleeved hand disappearing under the waves.

Bond lit a Raleigh and whispered to the gasping Dane. "I made the seven-ten split—and they split, too. It's all over, professor. Dr. Ernst Holzknicht is dead."

17

Games Xerox People Play

Another stroke of luck.

The well-proportioned masseuse, into whose ground-floor cubicle Bond had dragged the giant, informed the bullet-riddled duo she was an intern who found it necessary to moonight at the Samarra to supplement her meager income. From a case she took a thin, delicate instrument, inserted it into the band of scar tissue around Feldspar s left leg and extracted the ugly, flattened Manchester-Schlesinger slug.

"Good-o!" Bond enthused. "Honey, you're a regular"— and he chuckled roguishly as he whipped in the sparkling pun—"*Yen* Casey!" (When she did not collapse from laughter, he attributed it to her unfamiliarity with top-drawer Western humor.) "Professor, it looks like you're going to be OK. I can see your eyes brimming with gratitude for the valorous deed I've just done, but save your thanks. Purchase an Israel Bond of a sizable amount to help keep the Middle East's sole true democracy hale and free and that'll be reward enough. I've got some loose ends to clear up—the safe return of your son, squaring things with the Japanese— but in the interim, you cab it back to the Psyche-Deli and tell Sanka TUSH's Mr. Big will menace his country no more. And now, honey, take that lump of iron out of me."

When they were alone, the masseuse plied her skill on Bond's thigh and so adroit were her cool fingers that he scarcely felt a twinge. What he did experience as she probed that sensitive area was a pleasurable tingle, a sudden tumescence that rivaled Everest in lofty grandeur, and then their lips were locked in an ore-smelting kiss; pores excited pores; teats teatillated teats, and they were on the verge of a climax that would have blown the long-lost continent of Atlantis out of the depths of the sea and deposited it on the boardwalk of Atlantic City, when Bond's exaltation was shattered by the materializing of Sarah in the steam of the *ofuro*.

Oh, Iz. You've been unfaithful again.

"All right, goddammit!" he swore, disengaging himself from the disappointed masseuse. He strode briskly to the apparition and shook his fist. "Baby, I'm a man with a man's needs. You've been avenged. The Nazi pig who did you in is now in Davy Jones's locker. Or, if that's overcrowded, in Peter Tork's, Micky Dolenz's or Mike Nesmith's." (*Gottenu!* Another shaft of brilliance! The block-busting one-liners were pouring out at an incredible rate!) "Sarah, I know you got a lousy break in New York. Dying can be an awfully traumatic experience. But I'm alive; my life has to go on. Certainly there must be a host of sexy shades floating around in your dimension you can certainly turn on with—Old Marley, Canterville, or if you dig kids, Casper. What I'm trying to say in the kindest possible way is—*Stop bugging me!*"

Two chilly lips bussed his cheek. *Adieu, Iz. Adieu forever.*

And that's that, Bond thought. Resuming his place at the side of the delectable maiden, he grinned. "Shall we get back to the earth-moving business? If we really make an effort we can heave Vietnam into the Bering Sea and make the world safe for democracy and Drew Pearson."

His cruel sensual mouth was bruising hers when—

"Bond! Aleph priority!" The voice of Schlomo Salvar crackled over the Krai-Cain syncraphone's Frequency Baze Tzaddik. "The embassy just received a frantic message for you from a Miss Katz. Says she's trapped in her Xerox suite by two TUSH-ys."

"I'm on the way, Schlomo. Over and out," Bond told his false sixth bedsock toe. "Honey, I know you must think you've run into an *ichi-ban* weirdo who goes around talking to clouds of steam and his toes, but there's no time to explain. Where's the phone?"

A call to Sanka produced a *Kyodo Kikaku* helicopter on the roof garden piloted by a Major Domo, a ramrod of an officer. "I am at your disposal, Mr. Bond. The Xerox facility is but a few minutes' flying time from here and its penthouse contains one of Tokyo's finest heliports."

"*Arigato domo,* Domo. Or, Domo, *domo arigato.* Or..." *Dammit! There's another powerhouse of a one-liner somewhere in that combination,* Bond thought, *but it's escaped me for the moment. Anyway, this is no time for quipping when Kopy's in danger. Why has TUSH gone after her? And who's directing the show now that Holzknicht's out of the picture?*

The copter reached an altitude of two thousand feet in a few seconds and soon the garish, tinselly Ginza section was below them. The bars would be just about ready to close by now, Bond knew. Gorgeous hostesses, who'd been lighting cigarettes for tourists at three thousand yen an hour and promising paradise in their alluring winks, would be sneaking out through the back entrances to join their musician boyfriends while the drink-befuddled John Q. Travelers were being sobered up by tabs that could have financed insurrections in eight new African nations.

"Xerox ahead, Mr. Bond. Will you require my assistance?"

"No, thanks, Major Domo. After what I've been through, a couple of minor-league hoods will be Hostess cupcakes."

The craft hovered over the landing pad, then set down gently, though the gales from its rotors flung a trio of broom-wielding janitors over the edge. Bond watched them plummet like bundles of wet wash. "Don't feel bad about it, Domo. You've just created three new employment opportunities." He cursed himself for adopting so easily the Japanese indifference to death, but pushed it out of his mind when his feet hit the gravel.

He raced through the opulent surroundings, pausing only to filch a bottle of Johnnie Walker Black Label from a table on the terrace and give his insides a good heat treatment, then vaulted five steps at each bound down a stairway leading to the twentieth floor suite.

Kopy's oaken door was ajar. (*I wonder if she has a jar that's adoor,* he thought, in yet another demonstration of his fantastic wit.)

"Kopy! Kopy!" His voice echoed through her empty office.

"Iz." Her voice, so faint, so far away.

"Darling, what have they done to you?"

"Quickly, Iz. Through the green door!"

He barreled through the suite, upsetting lamps and worktables and a Ben Shahn masterpiece, the *Mona Schevitz,* until he found the green door, turned the handle and peered into a long, dimly lit corridor. "Kopy!"

"At the end of the hall, Iz! Hurry! I can't hold them off any longer!"

A shot shook the hallway.

Bond crouched, revved up into the old Bob Hayes breakaway sprint and traversed a hundred yards in 8.9 seconds. Another

scream—"Iz!"—sent a chill down his sensual, splendidly inter-
locked vertebrae.

He stopped on a dime at a black door over which a red
DANGER sign glowed dully. Picking up the coin and pocketing
it, he drove his massive shoulders into the door, cutting it down
like a blocking back paving the way for Gale Sayers, and hurtled
into utter blackness.

"Kopy! Kopy!"

Her voice was quite near now, curiously cool and mocking.
"That's fine, Iz. Just fine."

"Dammit! Are you playing games, baby? Where are you? It's
so dark I can't see my hand in front of my—"

Thump! On all sides he heard partitions hissing from the
ceiling to the floor. Bond flailed his fists and met cold metal. He
was in a trap. "What the hell..."

Kopy Katz's laugh rang out, frightening him with its
eeriness.

There was a flash as bright as an exploding sun. Something
titanic clobbered his head. Israel Bond pitched to the floor and
lay motionless.

18
Bondo
Limbo

"Someday you'll find it in your heart to forgive me for my little ruse," said Kopy Katz, placing the tenth icebag on the splitting head of Israel Bond. "I hated to do it this way, but, dammit, Iz, you kept ignoring my pleas."

He dragged on a Raleigh. "And you fired the shot, I gather."

"An added touch of drama, darling. It worked, didn't it? Oh, heaven, what a thrill to see you charging down that corridor like Lancelot to the rescue! My lovely, lovely knight." The raspberry lips blew suggestive zephyrs into his ear.

"Oy Oy Seven! Aleph priority!" Schlomo Salvar was back on his false sixth toe. "I've got to see you right away. All kinds of *mishigass** have been happening around here. First of all, your seven-foot Danish playmate stopped in, bought a ten-thousand-dollar Israel Bond as a token of his gratitude, fed me a few shots of some wicked brandy and left for Kyushu. Then Baron Sanka stormed in yammering bloody murder. He brought a copy of a video tape that's been airmailed to every major Japanese TV network from an undisclosed source in Europe. They've junked their regular schedule of programs to play it over and over. Turn on your TV set, then get here on the double."

Kopy pressed one of a row of buttons on her desk and a wall-size Sony hummed. The white dot spread; a Japanese announcer came on jabbering harshly and waving his arms in agitation.

"I'll translate, darling. He says the event we're about to witness occurred yesterday at a Common Market banquet in Brussels. It was filmed by an observer using a portable hand camera and supplied free of charge by 'A Friend of the Great

*   Craziness

Japanese People.' The man at the podium, he says, is Israel's Minister of Trade Hyman DeFlower. Recognize him?"

Bond did. "That's DeFlower, no doubt about it. *Gottenu!* He looks like he's stoned. Notice the glazed eyes, the St. Vitus-like *tzittering* of the lips."

"... able on this auspicious occasion to reveal for the first time a stunning breakthrough by a group of miniaturization specialists at our Technion Institute. Israel can now produce transistor radios of a quality far superior to anything emanating from Japanese laboratories—and cheaper, gentlemen, much cheaper. In the months to come we will reign supreme in this lucrative enterprise. Surely you cannot now deny my nation a Security Council membership in this prestigious organization..."

The Japanese commentator reappeared.

"He says, 'We shall replay the tape following a lengthy statement from Propaganda Minister Britt Kato.' Want to see more, Iz?"

"What for? Baby, as the razor manufacturer said when he accidentally dropped one of his shavers from a Cessna flying over Yankee Stadium: 'Now the Schick has really hit the fan!'"

"Iz, I'm going with you." The lovely Xeroxite replaced her silver chain and plunger with a copper one more suitable for casual afternoon wear and they took the elevator to a subbasement, where she tossed him the keys to a rakish, low-slung Castro convertible. "A wild thing, Iz. Quadruple carbs, twenty-four-volt Ruffing-Dickey battery, Sid Mark Three Pratt-Whitney engine capable of 188 nonmetric poods per dunam, and at night you can convert it into a very sexy couch."

The Castro whisked them to the embassy through streets ominously deserted. "I don't like this stillness," Bond said. "I haven't hit a single pedestrian in more than eighty blocks. Something's brewing."

A Miss Cilia Cohen, Salvar's curvaceous sabra secretary, led them to the diplomat's plush inner sanctum, where Sanka sat on a divan, seemingly under control, throwing spitballs at a large photograph of Theodor Herzl.

"Thank God you're here, Oy Oy Seven," said the short, bespectacled Salvar, rising to offer his hand. "I've been trying to convince the Baron there's been a horrible mistake but I'm afraid I haven't been getting through."

"The speaker in the video tape was Hyman DeFlower, is that not a fact, Izzy-san?"

"Yes, Baron, but he was wacked out of his *keppel*, couldn't you see that? Someone induced him to make that preposterous statement by some devilish means. Holzknicht, maybe."

"But your Danish friend apprised me of Holzknicht's death in Atami. Was Feldspar lying? Is this whole Holzknicht business a red herring cooked up between you and the Dane? The scrolls, the attack on me at the *ryokan*, all of it?"

"Dammit, Cocky-san!" Bond shook Sanka's shoulders. "Didn't I save your life in Beppu? Wasn't I wounded myself?"

Sanka sighed. "I don't know what to think, my friend. Salvar-san showed me a communication from your PM denying categorically Eretz Israel's plan to control the transistor market. But it hardly matters now. Our public is livid with rage, awaiting only the green light from the Diet to—"

Over the intercom shrilled Cilia Cohen. "Mr. Salvar! Come quickly! Look down the block! There's an army approaching the embassy."

Japanee no Jew!
Japanee no Jew!

The roar washed over the embassy.

Japanee no Jew!
Japanee no Jew!

There was a tinkling of glass. "Rocks—they're throwing rocks!" Miss Cohen was hysterical.

The four occupants of Salvar's chamber moved to a balcony overlooking the street. "The Sokka Datgai, Izzy-san," said Sanka with grim satisfaction. "They are coming in full force. I warned you my people would brook no more insults."

Bond, his gray eyes sweeping over the sea of blazing yellow faces, lit a Raleigh. "Where are the riot police?"

"They are on the way, Izzy-san. But I suspect they will not be too effective."

"You mean they'll have been told not to be too effective?"

Sanka's sneer was answer enough.

Japanee no Jew!
Japanee no Jew!

They were surging forward in phalanxes of two thousand, each preceded by a sound truck whose trained agitators were inflaming the marchers. "Hands off transistors! Japanee no Jew! Japanee are Japanee!"

A police truck pulled up, disgorged a paltry contingent of men in black uniforms and red combat hats. From the rear of the truck they pulled out four long steel riot poles and paired off into teams. They made a few halfhearted thrusts to contain the mob, grinning as they permitted themselves to be shoved back step by step.

Piff! Paff! Two rocks walloped Bond's head and in the mind-expanding flashes of agony he conceived a solution to this hairy situation.

The riot poles!

He recalled the docile, antlike behavior of the Japanese in the Atami nightclub as they'd scrambled to get into the limbo contest.

"Schlomo! I'm going down there. Send two of your best men after me, quickly! Tell them to grab one of the riot poles and pay attention to my spiel."

Bond leaped over the balcony railing to the soft, squooshy greensward, tore a bullhorn from the hands of one of the policemen and climbed onto the roof of the truck.

"Limbo! Let's do de limbo!" he yelled.

At first the demonstrators greeted his exhortation with a fusillade of missiles and he thought: *Anybody who dreams up a nutball scheme like this has rocks in his head. (Gottenu!* Another gem! If he got out of this alive he'd have to phone Earl Wilson and plant it in the "Wish I'd Said That" department of the column.)

His two embassy aides, strapping, bronzed sabras in light-blue Barbara Eden genie-jeans, had reached the scene, picked up an abandoned riot pole, stationed themselves at the ends, and the mob hushed, awaiting curiously the next move of this demented *gaijin.* Bond took advantage of the silence to bawl:

> *"Whether you've got a monko or chimbo,*
> *Jump in de line and let's do de limbo!"*

One of the agitators began to giggle. "Rimbo! Ret's do de rimbo!" The chant spread like wildfire to those in the rear. "Rimbo! Rimbo!"

"*Boocherim!*" Bond commanded his cohorts. "Move the stick away from the embassy. Where I go, you go."

"Rimbo! Rimbo!" The Sokka Datgai army was shouting and laughing now, and the first phalanx's ringleaders commenced to wiggle under the retreating pole, setting oif a wholesale rush.

"Run! Move it to the next street!" Bond thundered. And to his brain: *Create, create! Keep improvising Calypso verses and this crowd is Silly Putty in your long, tapering, sensual fingers.*

> "*Whether you Japanee or Jew,*
> *De limbo is de ting to do!*"

He broke into a gallop; so did his pole-bearing sabras and the joyous, jouncing hordes.

> "*Whether you be an uncle or tanteh,*
> *Do de limbo like Harry Belafanteh!*"

(A false rhyme, his ashamed brain admitted, but, hell, even heavyweight lyricists like Stephen Sondheim and Johnny Mercer would be copping out in a desperate game such as this!)

> "*I load de bananas on de sailing clipper,*
> *Daylight come 'n' me wanna go home.*
> *But I don't work when it comes Yom Kippur,*
> *Yomtov come 'n' me wanna stay home!*"

Gottenu! He'd been running and shouting for miles, it seemed. Where were they now? Yes, Shinjuku! The road-construction gangs were dropping their jackhammers, picks and shovels to join the ever-lengthening line that was causing the most horrendous traffic jam in Tokyo's history. And still more recruits were falling into the ranks—hostesses and their inebriated clientele from cheap bistros, burly cops deserting their beats, geishas jumping from pedicabs, and the scrawny individuals who'd been pulling them.

On limboed the caravan, Bond, his two puffing Israelis and hundreds of thousands of Japanese, including the Diet, which had ceased its debate on the new trade agreement with South Korea to become shrieking, ecstatic participants.

His body pleaded for a respite, but he ignored the heartrending entreaties of his nearly rent heart, wheezing lungs, tortured gristle and blunted shoulderblades. Onward! he urged them. The flag at the Israeli embassy will not be trampled this day! He croaked through the bullhorn in a fast-diminishing voice:

> *"Mom, you made a booboo, I shout!*
> *Don't like my daddy—please t'row him out!*
> *Daddy real nasty—that swine!*
> *I t'ink dat you married Joe Pyne!"*

They'd reached the Hakone area and presently were stumbling about in pine forests and game preserves, past ski lodges, into icy mountain streams. The embassy aides finally faltered and sank to their knees and relinquished the hundred-pound steel rod to Bond, who, without missing a beat, held it a foot from the ground to allow another few thousand or so to squeeze through on their bellies, then steeled his body for the last grueling leg of the contest.

On the summit of Mount Fuji, aglow in the roseate sunset, the limbo dance ended. Bond looked at the exhausted Japanese strewn about like clothespins on the trail, turned his eyes upward to his Maker and whispered in hoarse reverence:

> *"Lord, who made me nimble; Lord, who made me quick,*
> *I thank thee from my heart for dat good ol' limbo*
> *   shtick!"*

19

"Israel Bond Is Dead"

Major Domo, who'd been ordered by Sanka to track Bond from the copter, picked him up at Fuji's sixth station and ferried him to the embassy lawn. He limped past the adoring Cilia Cohen into Salvar's office, to be met by Kopy, whose abel-green eyes held a deep concern.

"Iz, thank heaven you're back. Schlomo's gone off the deep end. He started acting peculiar a while ago; a glaze came over his eyes and he sounded sort of, well, mechanical. He told Sanka he could straighten out all the misunderstanding if Sanka could get him an audience with the Emperor. Said he had new information proving Eretz Israel's innocence. He was so persuasive Sanka agreed. And he said he had a gift that would warm the Emperor's heart."

"A gift?"

"The Emperor is a marine-biology buff. Loves to add exotic specimens to his collection. Schlomo showed us a cute little tropical feller called a Ribicoff Rarity, which is spawned only in a certain stream in Connecticut, then spends the rest of its life trying to swim to the Indian Ocean. As you might imagine, darn few of 'em ever make it."

"Sounds damn fishy to me," Bond said, scoring minimally in the humor department. "I've got to get to the palace on the *double* double!"

He leaped back onto the lawn and caught Domo about to take off.

"This is most irregular, Mr. Bond. Landing on the grounds of the Son of Heaven's residence requires the highest security clearance."

"Dommit, Damo!" he swore and the hip Major cackled at Bond's rib-tickling play on his name. (Another socko ad lib! Who'd get this one? Jack O'Brian? Charles McHarry? Robert Sylvester? Even his straight lines were registering mega-boffs on the laugh meter.) "Forget the red tape, Major. If you refuse me you'll forevermore be known as Japan's Benedict Arnold."

The intensity in his expression won Domo over. "Hop in, Mr. Bond."

They came in fast over the Imperial Hotel, the palace moat, populated by huge golden-red carp, the high wall of brownish-gray boulders, then skimmed over gingkos, pines and brilliant clumps of cherry blossoms.

Crack! Crack! Bullets flew up from the carbines of a band of guards deployed into a human shield at the archway to the Imperial reception room. *Thwack!* Domo caught one in his shoulder, but bravely stayed at the controls and brought the craft to a jolting stop.

He staggered out, ignoring the blossoming patch on his jacket, and shouted something to the guards. "They'll pass you, Mr. Bond. Go!" Then he fell on his back.

Bond dropped a life-sustaining Excedrin into the gaping mouth. "Chew it, Domo." He ran through the arch down a tiled walkway, under a torii gate, and dived through a screen, landing catlike on his feet a couple of yards from the gold-and-black-robed Emperor of Japan, who was squinting into a glass tank held by the top-hatted, white-tie-and-tailed Salvar. "This, Your Majesty," the diplomat intoned, "contains—"

"Death! Caveat Emperor!" He flattened Salvar with a quarter-strength South Korean karate cut to the midriff taught him by a Seoul-brother, made a sensational shoestring catch of the falling tank and raised it high.

The cry of "Death!" in the presence of the Emperor started the adrenal coursing in Sanka, who whipped out a black Wembley-Vicar, got Bond in its sights and squeezed the trigger three times.

"Sanka, you fool," muttered Bond, pressing the long, tapering fingers of his left hand against his punctured abdomen.

With a moan he cocked the fish tank in his hand like a football and let it fly in a Bart Starr-bullet through the screen. He smiled thinly and toppled to the carpet.

A red ball artichoked into the sky; there was the oppressive smell of Calgonite, and fragments of the torii gate flew into the room.

"By the belly of Buddha!" screamed Sanka. "There was a Calgonite charge in that tank! Oy Oy Seven!" He went down on his knees before the Israeli. "The royal physician, quickly!"

"Cocky." Bond's voice was almost inaudible. "Got a last great one-liner for you, *boychikl*. It's adieu to espionage. I... just... haven't... got... the"—there was a ghost of a chuckle as he got in the punch line—"stomach for it... any more...." The sensual, vein-free eyelids rolled over the gray eyes.

Sanka felt for the pulse, caught the tiniest of throbs. Then nothing.

"Your Majesty," he said, bowing slowly and gracefully. "Your life has been saved by the greatest practitioner of espionage the world has ever known. It was his gesture of *sayonara* to you, to me and to the people of Japan. The royal physician will be of no use now. Israel Bond is dead."

20

Mr. Tambourine Man

In his Cathouse of the August Tea suite, Baron Cockimamiyama Sanka concluded his votive offerings to his household gods, reciting a haiku.

> *"I do not fear death.*
> *What I do fear is that it may*
> *not be permanent."*

"Excellent!" said his lifelong friend Count Iyama Pishaka, of the Foreign Office. "A verse of our seventeenth-century haiku master Bassho?"

"No. Buck Rogers of the 25th century." Sanka lit a Raleigh, his 10,718th since he had pulled the trigger that meant "thirty" for Israel Bond. The coupons would be sent to M. in Jerusalem so they could be credited to Bond's account. "It is good of you to stand by me in my final hour on this mortal coil. Have you prepared the sword?"

"*Hai.* I have dipped it from hilt to tip in Binaca, a Japanese potion. Your death will not only be agonizing, but fragrant. Allow me to place the ceremonial robe upon you." Slipping the richly brocaded garment over the chunky shoulders, he asked, "Have you completed your will?"

"You will find it on a scroll near the gods. The twenty-seven million yen I have accumulated from years of dedicated defalcation will fund a number of causes dear to the heart of Oy Oy Seven—the Committee for the Purchase of Israel Bonds, of course, and the United Jewish Appeal, the Jewish National Fund for the Reforestation of the East Bronx, the Joe E. Lewis Foundation for World Peace through Alcoholism, the Jewish Home for the Uninspired and so forth."

"What crosscut have you chosen, Baron? The classical style of the *daimyo*[*] Haidan Sikko, which begins at the wisdom teeth and ends in the colon?"

"I have ruled out that one, my friend. Because of an operation I underwent two years ago, I have only a semicolon. No, I have decided upon a modern technique created by the founder of our national sound-recording system, Muzaki—from anus to larynx, from Memphis to St. Joe, wherever the four winds blow." *How Izzy-san, who had been so enamored of humor, would have appreciated that one,* Sanka sighed.

In his mind's eye he could still see the El Al jet with its sad cargo, the simple pine box wrapped in a giant-size trenchcoat (a sentimental touch requested by Miss Katz), winging to Eretz Israel, where the state funeral would be held.

Because of the unusual nature of Bond's passing and the need for complete secrecy, the simplest sort of ceremony had been conducted at the Jewish Community Center of Tokyo, attended by only a handful of mourners: Kopy Katz in a black chain and plunger, and her escort, a humpbacked, bearded man in dark glasses she'd introduced as her father; the embassy people, including a handcuffed, red-eyed Schlomo Salvar, who'd been permitted to attend by a special order from Sanka; Ginza-Burg, a yarmulke jammed over his cabby's cap, and Sanka, Pishaka and Propaganda Minister Kato, who'd been sent to express the official grief of a stunned Emperor.

Ginza-Burg had said the Kaddish, the Prayer for the Dead, and added an affecting aside. "I gotta leave real *schnell*. There's a fare in my cab and the meter's still running, but I just wanna say this. If there's a shining spot that's like a Kosher Camelot, that's where this wonderful warrior is right now. *Olav Hashalom*—may he rest in peace."

An unexpected visitor had come to the front of the chapel, a little man in a white frockcoat, string tie and thirty-gallon Pedernales River sombrero.

"Folks, I'm Oral Vincent Graham, the traveling evangelist, and it was my privilege to have known Mr. Bond during two of his adventures. When his boss lady in Jerusalem learned I was in Japan spearheading my latest crusade, she cabled me and asked me to say a few words that might comfort you in this moment

[*]   Feudal noble

of tragedy. During my oration there'll be a tambourine passed among you. Any offering you'd care to make will be deeply appreciated. If you find yourselves without coins or folding money, just throw in your credit cards. We accept 'em."

He lit a long, odoriferous cigar, leaned against the casket and spoke his piece:

> *"Ashes to ashes, dust to dust,*
> *If you don't like my figure,*
> *Take your hands off my bust."*

He hemmed and hawed for a few seconds, clearly embarrassed.

"You'll pardon that unfortunate lapse into childish doggerel, folks. Funny how them little outhouse-wall poems come back to you at a time like this." He extinguished the cigar on the casket and resumed.

"We all came from Clay—or Muhummad Ali, if ye subscribe to another faith—and back to Clay we must go. Did not John the Baptist sayeth upon discovering a precious stone in the waters of the Jordan: 'Holy mackerel! It's Sapphire!' And, yea, unto ye I say, did not Ezekiel crieth when he saw the wheel, 'Number five on the black!'

"The Lord freed Sam Sheppard; he shall not want. Yes, let he who is without stones cast the first sin. For out of the mouths of babes comes Pablum and pacifiers. And Nashua fit de battle at Pimlico and the odds came a-tumblin' down.

"Be that as it may. Ye shall know the truth and it will make you sick.

"You've got to walk that lonesome valley; you've got to walk it by yourself. So walk on through the wind; walk on through the rain; for a rose must remain in the sun or the rain or its lovely promise won't come true. I know that Israel Bond's indomitable spirit is walking right now through that lonesome valley, the wind and the rain and those crappy waterlogged roses, and he'll never stop, though he's scorned and covered by scars, until he climbs every mountain, fords every stream and reaches the unreachable stars.

"I thank you." Oral Vincent Graham had taken the cigar butt from the casket, relit it by scratching a match on the seat of his pants and poked through the tambourine.

"Cheap crowd," someone heard him mutter.

Even the Japanese observers, who had been trained all their lives to conceal their deepest emotions, had wept quarts of tears.

A curious incident had occurred as Sanka got in the line moving past the casket to pay his last respects. Miss Katz, who surprisingly was dry of eye, shook his hand warmly, but her bent old father cursed at him and landed a sharp kick in the *Kyodo Kikaku* leader's groin. "You trigger-happy fascist bastard! When I think of that beautiful boy lying in there all shot up and all the women in the world who'll never know what true ecstasy is because of your precipitate action, I could—"

"Please, Dad," Miss Katz had said. "The Baron was only doing his duty, which was to safeguard the Emperor." She had then led the fractious codger away.

Now the sword was in Sanka's hand and finger. "Count Pishaka, please grant an old crony a last wish. Use every bit of your considerable influence to cool the temper of our people. Bond gave his life to prevent war. And while I as yet have not penetrated this mystery, I am certain his nation is not at fault. Give Major Domo the records of this case and tell him to institute a thorough investigation until the real culprits are in chains. And now, *sayonara*, Pishaka."

The men exchanged deep bows.

"Stop him!" The scream of Kopy Katz came through the paper screen.

"Let him do it already. I'm not going to make a career out of stopping this *schmuck* from doing himself in," said a familiar whimsical voice. "All right, I'll stop him. But it's the last time."

Kopy's father walked into the suite from the garden. He wrested the sword from Sanka and broke it over his knee, pulled off his beard and dark glasses, lit a Raleigh, removed his Chesterfield coat, to whose rear lining a pillow was fastened, then ignited his Chesterfield coat with his Raleigh. "Wish I could light my Raleigh with this Chesterfield" he muttered.

Baron Cockimamiyama Sanka's eyes rolled like marbles gone mad; he grasped at his throat and fainted dead away.

"Any spirits of ammonia around here, Count Pishaka?" said Israel Bond, stomping on his coat to stop the fire.

21

Not All Lox Is Smoked Salmon

A pinch of *chrain* in each nostril brought Sanka back to the land of the living, though he did not speak for many minutes. With eyes wide as those in a Walter Keane portrait, he stared at the dark, cruelly handsome, broadly grinning Oy Oy Seven.

"Sorry I kicked ye in the old *baytzim* back in the chapel, Cocky-san, but you must admit I had justification. When you run into a guy who's just killed you, you have to do something positive or lose your self-respect. Friends like you I don't need; I'd rather have nonviolent enemies." He softened and wrapped a sinewy arm around the Baron. "I'm kidding, old Nip. Truth is I've gotten fond of you. I don't blame you for seeing red. If something appeared to be threatening my PM, I'd do the same."

"I saw you take three W-V bullets in the stomach. I saw you expire. I saw you placed in a coffin and flown to your homeland."

Bond passed his pack of Raleighs around. "This will prove I'm no ghost. Here's my latest haiku. Dig.

> *A good sex life stops*
> *mental illness. Fight a*
> *crackup with a shackup!*

OK, Cocky?"

"*Hai.* Only Israel Bond could be so profoundly romantic. But how—"

"Years ago in the Orient," Bond interjected, "I learned the secret of clouding men's minds from the Mongolian, Takka Ah Shonda, the last of the red-hot lamas. Oh, you tell 'em, Kopy. It's a shade too involved for me."

Kopy Katz inhaled and heaved her magnificent mammaries. "Israel Bond did die. At least an exact duplicate of him died after leading the Sokka Datgai on the limbo chase. A short time ago, I, who've been living in constant trepidation that sooner or later his Oy Oy Seven number would be up, lured him into the 'Black Room,' a secret lab in the rear of my Xerox office, and copied him—molecule for molecule, subatomic particle for subatomic particle. While Iz lay around reading *Commentary* and eating boxes of Good 'N Plenty, his duplicate was pulling off the usual Bondian superfeats. The 'Black Room' itself is the inside of an experimental Xerox that nobody in the organization, not even Mr. Sol Linowitz, knows about—the Xerox-Googol-Plex. Without going into too much detail, it utilizes transuranic elements in an instantaneous but controlled nuclear process. That's what caused the flash and gave you the headache, darling. You were in the epicenter of a mini-H-bomb explosion. It gave the Ginza section a helluva shake, but this town's always being rocked by minor earthquakes so nobody paid much attention. When I received the formula, I'd originally intended to use the 'Black Room' to duplicate another Xerox. Think of the billions I could have saved the corporation by duplicating new machines instead of building them from scratch. But"—her voice lowered—"I fell in love, Iz, and because of that I did something far worse than betray my country or my faith. I—I betrayed Xerox."

Bond ran a loving hand over the oval face. "I appreciate it, baby. But you said you 'received' the formula. You mean you didn't whip it up yourself?"

"Gentlemen and Iz, I'm no slouch in the gray-matter league. Only nine other people in the world wear this insignia." She fondled the chain and plunger. "I won't go through the whole list, but among them are the fabled little old colored shoeshine boy who wrote not only all of Irving Berlin's songs, but Richard Rodgers', too; Morris Berenbaum of Thiokol, who discovered that certain forms of German measles are caused by viruses hatched in the motors of Volkswagens; David Susskind, whose main goal is discovering his own possibilities; Yonkel Schreiber-Burns of the Rand Corporation, who is well on the way to creating eternal life, as soon as he gets over the last little hurdle—how to stop people from dying. We Alta Zeyda Kapplans keep in constant touch by mail and ham radio, swap our latest theories. The formula for the Xerox-Googol-Plex is the brainchild of the *ichi-ban* AZK of us all. Your Holzknicht couldn't carry this man's bedroom slippers."

"Who is he?" said an interested Count Pishaka.

"A man with a confirmed IQ of 666—the little devil—and, I'm proud to say, a fellow Jew. He's quite mad, of course, but he periodically breaks out of it to bedazzle the rest of us. His name is Lavi HaLavi."

Bond turned his sensual gray eyes away so they could not see the mist gathering. "I cursed him for failing me and all he's done is save my life—again."

Now it was Sanka's turn to be the comforter. "Izzy-san, this is no time to weep. This is a joyous occasion. Tomorrow we shall work hand in finger to corral these malefactors, but now let us celebrate. We shall have a feast fit for a king—an Alan King!"

Gottenu! Bond thought. *My scintillating wit has rubbed off on the Baron. He's damn near as fast on the uptake as I am.*

Sanka phoned Ginza-Burg, gave him a series of instructions and hung up. "The food is on the way, my friends. Blintzes from Charlie Mano's, mouth-watering sukiyaki from Kathy, one of the mama-sans at the VIP Bar, and a conglomeration of Ann Dinken's best Jewish delicacies. In the meantime let us make merry."

They sat in the Lotus position around Sanka's table, singing boisterously like children at a campfire. Bond and Kopy taught their hosts some jolly Stern Gang dynamiting songs; the Japanese predictably sang "Sakura"; then Sanka opened the curtains of a wicker cage and commanded a chorus of crickets to chirp in foxtrot rhythm and they danced—Kopy with Sanka, Bond with Pishaka—until they fell in laughing exhaustion on the tatami.

Ipanema chose that moment to stagger into the suite with a carton on her slim shoulder. She dumped its contents on the table, which cracked under the burden of the thousand-yen notes. "Ipanema keeping her bargain, Izzy-san."

"Who is this girl?" said an irritated Kopy.

Think fast! Bond told his brain. "A waif I used to send CARE packages to in the 1950s when she was in an Osaka orphanage. She vowed she'd work her tail off to repay me, darling."

Sanka tactfully sent the maiden away to commit suicide. "And here, my friends, is Ginza-Burg."

The cabby, his face alight in an infectious smile, sauntered through the screen bearing three large trays. *"Essen! Meer gayen essen, kinderlach!"*[*]

He set one tray on the floor and peeled off the tinfoil coverings.

Kopy's nose wrinkled. "Lox."

"And bagels to you, luv," Bond said. "Seems to me we've done this verbal byplay before. This is going to be one dull marriage if all you do is say 'lox.'"

"Silly." She held his hand. "Oh, yes, I remember now. I said it on the cliff, didn't I? But that was when that poor little workman dropped the cylinder and Feldspar got all hot and bothered. I didn't mean smoked salmon that time, Iz. Lox is also a bit of scientific slang. I meant to pursue it further, but, as I recall, Feldspar practically stepped on my conversation."

"What did you mean?" A sudden hardness was back in Bond's eyes.

"Lox means liquid oxygen. You know, the stuff they use in guided missiles."

---

[*]　Chow, chow, bambinos!

22
Loves Of
A Bond

"Faster! Faster!" Bond begged Major Domo, now at the controls of Baron Sanka's Lear jet.

"We are already at 650 mph, Mr. Bond. Beppu Airport has cleared us for touchdown in six minutes."

"The hell with Beppu. From there it's another two hours by car to Shimonoshima and we can't afford the time. I want you to cut your speed, come in over the cliffs and we'll bail out."

"A dicey proposition. The currents may catch you and blow you far out to sea."

"A chance we'll have to take."

"May I give my belated thanks for the remedy you forced into me in the Imperial garden, Mr. Bond?"

"Don't thank me, Domo. Thank Excedrin. And remember—only Excedrin can take away the pain caused by aspirin. Kopy, you ever jumped before?"

"Loads of times," said the researcher. "When I was a teener we lived in northern New Jersey and I belonged to the Teterboro Airport Skydiving Club. It was such fun free-falling and trying to avoid Arthur Godfrey's plane. Give me another minute, though. I haven't finished mixing the stuff."

"Are you sure it's necessary?"

"Lavi HaLavi thinks so. It's his idea. Simple but absolutely brilliant as usual. I radioed him at Foam Rubber Acres in Galilee and, thank heaven, I caught him during the five minutes of each hour that he's rational. The psychiatrist told me he spends the rest of the time riding on a rocking horse, crying, 'Half a league, half a league, half a league onward!' then looks behind and asks, 'Where the hell are the other 599? If you think I'm going into the mouth of hell alone, you're crazy!'"

An improvement at that, Bond thought. *At least he's out of the sandpile.* "What else did he say?"

"If TUSH has managed to assemble a nuclear missile under our noses, you know the target. By now Lavi has alerted the Ministry of Defense to evacuate the citizenry of the Tel Aviv-Jerusalem area, though I don't think that'll do much good. It could reach Eretz Israel in twenty-five minutes. Maybe it's already been fired. If not"—and she held up a test tube of a pinkish liquid like a proud mother doting on her newborn—"there's still a chance." Kopy unscrewed a cap on her silver AZK plunger, poured the brew into it and recapped it. "A missile uses thousands of gallons of hydrocarbon fuel piped into it from storage tanks. If I can just—"

"Shimonoshima ahead," said Major Domo. "You'll find the chutes on the wall near the door."

Bond helped Kopy into the harness, worked his way into his own chute and lit a Raleigh. By now the Baron should have rounded up his *Kyodo Kikaku Kommando* forces, a top-secret cadre of hardened battlers, and perhaps their copters were leaving Honshu this very second, he hoped. But for the next couple of hours he and Kopy would have to carry the ball alone.

He signaled to Domo to pull the door switch, yelled "Cochise!" (Bond considered himself an innovator, not a follower, and besides, he'd always felt Geronimo had been overexposed) and hurled himself into a brilliant, sun-splashed sky. Kopy picked up the cue— "Crazy Horse!" —and jumped after him.

The sentinel on the cliff picked up the pair of vanilla-ice-cream-cone-shaped objects in his binoculars and spoke hurriedly into his walkie-talkie. *"Achtung!* Two interlopers in the sky. One of them is *Der Jude."*

"Acknowledged. Deploy the men, Eisswess. Take Bond alive." In the largest tent Professor Igneous Feldspar sipped daintily from a glass of Liebfraumilch. "So," he said to the naked, sex-crazed woman thrashing about on her cot, "your hero comes like an avenging angel of the Lord. Run to him, you disgusting trollop. It will provide me a bit of entertainment."

"Bond! Bond! Bond!" shrieked Magma Feldspar and ran out into the sunshine.

Even from her dory a mile from shore and a thousand feet below, the keen-eyed Ama maiden knew it was her lover alighting on the cliff. "Those thighs, those shoulders, that cruelly handsome profile," she sobbed. "It can be no other."

Go-Down Mikimoto drove the oars toward the landing at a rate that would have left the racing shells of Princeton, Harvard and Dartmouth capsized in her boiling wake.

Bond hit the rocks first and his heart sank as he heard Kopy's "The wind's got me! Help, Iz!" A sudden, treacherous current was, as Domo had feared, impelling her seaward. "Kopy!" he called helplessly.

His ears caught the grating of feet and he spun, tearing his Hontze-Ganendel automatic from his Neiman-Marcus shoulder holster. It was one of two guns he'd hastily requisitioned from Sanka's private arsenal. The other was a Beretta, stuck into his cummerbund.

He crouched behind one of the many *yoni* bushes. Into view stalked six truncheon-wielding Norwegians, part of the bunch he'd met earlier, but they'd exchanged their black sweaters for polo shirts and their exposed inner arms bore the telltale tattoo—jackboots kicking naked buttocks. Norwegians, hell, he thought. They're TUSH-ys! And while they might be great shakes as Buddha-builders, they're without question missile technicians as well.

"He landed in this vicinity, Pieterdeter," said one of them in a Rhinelander dialect. "We need not concern ourselves with the girl. I saw her swept into the ocean. But why should he have come virtually unaided?"

"He rather fancies himself as a superhero, I am told, my dear Eisswess," said the contumelious Pieterdeter.

Bond ground his cavity-free teeth, shoved the Hontze-Ganendel back into its holster and flung himself out of the hiding place, snarling, "S for Solomon, H for Halavah, A for Abraham, Z for Zangwill, A for Abraham *noch amool*, and M for Moses! SHAZAM, you Nazi bastards!"

He crashed like a boulder into the sextet, his bronzed arms, elbows, stiffened fingers and steel shafts of legs dealing lethal blows to salient sectors of their anatomies.

Eisswess died at once of a crushed windpipe. The nose of Pieterdeter was mashed into strawberry Jell-O. A toe emasculated one Herr Hauptnerr.

The remaining threesome, who'd been less forcefully battered by Bond's Ugandan elephant charge, got in close and drummed their truncheons against his stomach and right shoulder, reopening a few of the old combat wounds in the latter location. Claret gushed forth like the geysers of Beppu, but he took a mighty breath and his chest expanded to twice its normal size, hurling them to the ground. Though he would have preferred to finish these lice by hand, he decided to conserve his fading power. Liberating the Hontze-Ganendel again, he blasted away at the whimpering Germans—the characteristic *ver gehargit! ver gehargit!* report shaking the earth as the heavy-caliber slugs blew them down. They lay splayed out in various attitudes of death.

"I must say I like your attitudes," he flipped and patted his back for the bon mot. Wondering vaguely which would hold out longer, his strength or his humor, he jogged toward the tent city, his sensual gray eyes seeking the perfidious Danish giant who'd led him down the garden path so often in this puzzling affair.

Kopy landed on her back, the weight of her drenched chute several times pulling her under, but she finally undid the harness and freed herself. Coughing, regurgitating brine, plankton and a medium-size langouste, and arching her willowy body, she began a choppy crawl to the shore. *Gottenu! It'll take me an hour to reach him,* she lamented.

Then she saw the boat. "Help! Please help!"

Go-Down Mikimoto had no intention of stopping for this *gaijin* woman, whom she had seen parachuting down in the company of her man, but she had a guilty second thought: *Perhaps he loves this woman. I cannot do anything to hurt him, although rescuing her may shut me out of his life forever.*

"Give me your hand," said Go-Down and lifted the fatigued researcher into the dory. "You are his woman, is it not so?"

The Xeroxite gave her rescuer a knowing appraisal. "You love him, too."

Go-Down did not answer, but her bobbing Adam's apple betrayed her emotions and Kopy knew it was so.

"You poor, sweet little lady," Kopy said, drawing the trembling Ama girl to her breast. "We've got to help him together. He's in there alone against—God knows what. And I've a mission of my own."

As Go-Down rowed, Kopy explained what had to be done.

"Oh, but I know Shimonoshima quite well, Miss Katz," affirmed Go-Down. "Only yesterday I was at the site of the com-

pleted Great Herrosukka Buddha. Some of the Japanese workmen are relatives of mine and permitted me to pray before it."

"And you didn't see anything that looked like large tanks?"

"No, Miss Katz. But if these evil ones are as clever as you say,
they might have concealed them in any number of large caves
and built underground pipelines to your supposed missile. Yet
I saw no missile. The only large edifice standing is the mighty
Buddha itself."

Kopy Katz swore at herself in Yiddish, then said, "I'm a fool
to the tenth power, Go-Down. It's so damn obvious. The missile
is inside the Buddha!"

"Then we must kill it at its source, Miss Katz. As a child
I played often in the labyrinths of Shimonoshima and still
remember many of the passageways. I shall lead you through
them for his sake."

"You're an OK gal, Go-Down," said Kopy Katz. "Now get your
stroke rate up to 150 per minute and let's go spelunking."

They smiled at each other, these two gorgeous, naked
women, so different in background and appearance, but, like the
colonel's lady and Judy O'Grady, sisters under the skin.*

---

*   A little cheap emotion never hurts any book.—S.W.

23
The Quest Ends

Bond, crawling on his swollen belly like a deadly puff adder, racked up Nazis seven and eight in a noiseless fashion. They stood on guard several yards from Feldspars tent, smoking and chatting unconcernedly, and by the time they heard the *yoni* twigs snapping under his advancing body he'd pressed the button of his mezuzah to send the two Molochamovis-B-tipped needles whizzing into their necks.

Good-o! Ten left, counting the Dane, or rather the German, which he certainly had to be. But who was Feldspar or whatever his name was? He'd familiarized himself with the entire TUSH dossier since the organization's inception in the mid-'50s and had etched into his memory the facts concerning every one of its major operatives, all of whom had been taken in the counter-attack in Sahd Sakistan—except the late Holzknicht, who'd lammed to the U.S. None of them, either living or dead, came close to approximating the outré physique of Feldspar.

Lost in thought, he did not realize he himself was being stalked. Just as he tippy-toed to the giant's tent, there was a rush of air, the slapping of naked feet and—*whump!*—he was cut down by a flying tackle.

"Bond! I need you! I need you!" wailed the aroused Magma Feldspar, whose satiny, powerful arms were locked around his ankles.

The commotion brought the Nazi scientists on the run and the great golden hand pushed aside the flap and Feldspar lurched out on the giraffe legs, a Luger cocked at Bond's head.

"One more time!" Magma implored him, her greedy hands scrabbling at his manhood. "One more time!"

Bond said, "OK," and absentmindedly began to vocal-bop the famous coda from Basie's "April in Paris."

"No, you lamebrain! I mean, take me, take me!"

"Excellent!" said Igneous Feldspar. "You have served me well, you Danish bitch. Now, *auf Wiedersehen*." He swung the Luger around and fired. Magma Feldspar's head blew up in a red cloud.

"You bastard—killing your own wife," Bond swore and in a lightning draw aimed the Beretta at the spot between the giant's ice-blue eyes.

Feldspar did not blink an eyelash. He seemed amused. "Fire, Oy Oy Seven."

Bond squeezed the Beretta's trigger.

Nothing.

The damn gun had jammed.

"It is a matter of record that all Berettas jam in crucial situations, Herr Bond. It serves you right for selecting a ladies' gun."

Thonk! Klonk! Frick! Frack! His aides' truncheons landed on Bond's head and the secret agent was out cold.

"Welcome to BO minus forty, Herr Bond." Triumph wreathed the pasty face of Igneous Feldspar.

"Which has no connection with Lifebuoy, I bet," Bond said. He gave his pulpy head a shake. It seemed three sizes too big. His hands were clasped in front of him, turning blackish from the biting straps of saranoflex. "Forty minutes to blastoff, eh?"

"*Sehr gut.* Your mentality is unimpaired by the piddling blows. This is a shining moment in your life, Herr Bond. Your hyperactive heart should be leaping for joy."

"What do you mean, you murdering swine?"

The giant blew Muriel smoke into Bond's face. "Tut, tut, my friend. Is that any way to speak to the man you've traveled thousands of miles to confront? I am Dr. Ernst Holzknicht."

24
Neck
Check

Well, why not? Bond asked himself. *There were two of* me. *Yet the Holzknicht who went over the roof of the Samarra bathhouse looked like the old, despised model. An actor? An expendable, low-grade TUSH-y made up to simulate* lieber *Ernst?*

"Let me begin at the beginning," Holzknicht said.

Bond had no bone to pick with that approach. It was one his own logical mind might have chosen. "Please do."

"When I fell from the Empire State Building and bounced off the foam-rubber skull of King Kong into the Lowenbrau beer truck, I suffered a multiplicity of injuries. But in the undaunted spirit of true Nazism I hung on and when the truck wended its way through Manhattan's Yorkville section I tapped on the window, got the bewildered driver's attention and paid him well to assist me into a certain apartment building on East Eighty-fourth Street."

"Fritz Kuhn Towers, no doubt," Bond broke in. "We've had it watched sporadically. Loaded with your kind of maniacs."

Holzknicht let that disclosure pass. "In my heart was a consuming hatred for you and Eretz Israel which, if transformed into heat ergs, could have turned the polar cap into a Congo rain forest. I lay in my bed, broken and spent, but my brain was as sharp as ever. It told me that you would eventually turn up in Japan to seek the kind of sinister intrigue that can only be found here."

"The historical verity," Bond half whispered.

"Ah, someone in your M 33 and 1/3 has also read every novel of espionage ever written. Yes, the historical verity. Well put."

"BO minus thirty-five," trumpeted a voice from the walkie-talkie on Holzknicht's cot.

"Why did you have to go through this elaborate folderol involving the Japanese? A few ounces of your *barbarella* toxin dumped by night into the major reservoirs of Eretz Israel would have accomplished your task."

"Too simple, Herr Bond." He sighed, a Heidelberg dean trying to explain the principles of Clausewitz to a child brought up on Bomba the Jungle Boy. "Like so many great men who reach middle age, I am afflicted by accidie, which can only be overcome by spurring on my mind to create concepts of infinite subtlety such as 'Operation Alienation,' which sought to destroy the spirit of Judaism by removing its most significant element—Jewish food."

"You damn near succeeded," Bond grunted.

"After my wounds healed and I'd decided to come to the Orient, it became necessary to alter my appearance. I administered local anesthesia to myself and operated on myself, replacing my fine German hands with these steam shovels—one at a time, of course—and adding eighteen inches to my legs by means of bone grafts. A lesser man would have been squeamish, but we of the Master Race are something more than lesser men. More or less. I softened the angular lines of my face with plastic surgery to achieve this bovine pastiness, inserted ice-blue contact lenses, let my black hair grow and went to Mr. Schatzi, the East Berlin hair stylist, who curled it and lightened it with Summer Blonde by Clairol. My next step was a change of nationality. In Copenhagen I bribed a minor official to create a new identity for me, then induced a bar slut to marry me. I knew our paths would cross, but you would be seeking Ernst Holzknicht, not a stumbling blond giant with a wife. I duped Magma into believing I was under Holzknicht's influence via a faked telephone call, for it was my plan that she fall in love with you and in an intimate moment 'spill the beans,' as the Americans say.

"It has been a game of cat and mouse, Oy Oy Seven, and I have not been the mouse. How I laughed inside when your noble heart was touched by the pathetic, ungainly figure of Igneous Feldspar and his crushing secret sorrow. Of course, Knute Feldspar never existed. And, by the bye, I was the German officer responsible for the death of your beloved Helvig Rolvig.

"I obtained the approbation of the Japanese to carry on my excavation project and brought over the 'Norwegians,' for I was determined to have an ace in the hole, the missile, should all else fail. They were former members of the *Führer*'s V-2 echelon, who escaped Europe through our underground network to eventually turn up in Egypt to work for the Cairo Colonel. I borrowed them from a secret missile base in central Egypt.

"In the meantime I set into motion a series of incidents calculated to inflame the Japanese against Eretz Israel. The first was the trawler. In a Greek waterfront cafe its crew was fed coffee into which was mixed Hypno-70, a drug which has a hypnotic effect upon the taker lasting from a day to many months, depending upon the amount ingested. The *Blintz Charming* was cleared for passage through Suez by the Colonel and made its attack upon the Imperial gunboat. My second ploy, the destruction of the JAL jet, was foiled by you because of Aw Gee Minh's petty desire for revenge. Had I known you were on that flight I would have ordered him to destroy another.

"The scrolls—faked, of course—were prepared by an Arab scholar versed in Biblical lore. Although they were inscribed on papyrus treated by a special process to make them appear pristine, I dared not let a true expert scrutinize them, so I insisted they remain in the cave. My mistake was chatting about them in the presence of Nikko Tee-Yin, whose consequent suspicious behavior convinced me he was from the *Kyodo Kikaku*. Before Yaynu eliminated him, he had already gotten word to his *ichi-ban*, who cabled that he wanted copies, so I agreed to the Xeroxing by Miss Katz.

"Once I knew Sanka's interest was aroused, I was afraid to have an intelligence operative as shrewd as the Baron snooping around, so I ordered Skwato to tag him to Tokyo and liquidate him. By this time you were his ally and foiled Skwato's attempts in Tokyo and Beppu.

"The other major provocations were also drug-inspired. One of my agents slipped it into Hyman DeFlower's borscht in Brussels. I myself gave it to Schlomo Salvar in brandy."

"Put two more foils on my tally sheet, *Herr Doktor*," Bond said. "I led the demonstrators away from the Israeli embassy, then returned to prevent the Emperor's death. I imagine the Ribicoff Rarity was a mere goldfish done up by a pop artist."

"I learned of the failure of the latter scheme when I turned on television. Instead of fiery declarations of war it was carrying such drivel as *Shogun Fight at the Kamakura Korral*, *My Three Samurai* and *The Dog from U.N.C.L.E.* And today's papers were peculiarly devoid of scathing editorials," the Nazi said.

"Good-o! Sanka, Count Pishaka and Minister Kato have been suppressing the hotheads. Tell me, if all these gambits had worked, how would the Japanese have reached Israel?"

"Certain circles in Red China and the U.S.S.R., who would like to see Eretz Israel go under, were prepared to wink at the squadrons of Imperial Japanese atom bombers flying over their respective territories, even to refuel them. There would have been a brief violation of Iranian air space, then they would have zeroed in over Arab states, who, of course, were more than happy to cooperate. Would they have minded the loss of a few hundred thousand out of their one hundred million if the Zionist state was at long last exterminated?"

"BO minus twenty-five, *Herr Doktor.*"

"You see, Herr Bond, I wanted you to survive the murderous inclinations of Yaynu and Frau Marlene. I knew that they, like the monk, so detested you they would disobey my orders, but I also felt you would luck through in your customary fashion.

"When you became my protector," he chuckled, "and insisted upon a showdown with Holzknicht, I was prepared for that exigency, too. The 'Holzknicht' you sent over the bathhouse with the Black Dragqueen was a robot, the idea for which was suggested by the remarkably lifelike Abraham Lincoln in the Illinois pavilion at the recent New York World's Fair."

"Of course. That accounts for the jerkiness of the mouth and hands, *Herr Doktor.*"

"*Ja.* I had ordered the Black Dragqueen to merely wound you as well as myself. I wanted to see how you, disarmed and bloodied, would dispose of your tormentors. Incidentally, I feel virtually no pain in these new legs." The Nazi suddenly jabbed his cigar end into Bond's cheek, held it there for a second that seemed an eternity. "A small repayment for the knife you hurled into me, *Jude.*"

Though nauseated by the stench of his burned flesh, Bond kept his cool. "Why did you keep me alive?"

"Because"—and Holzknicht peeked at his watch—"in less than twenty minutes I want you to witness that which you cannot prevent, the blastoff of a missile tipped with a multi-megaton warhead, and listen to a shortwave radio account of the flash from my colleagues at the Egyptian base in another twenty-five minutes. I want to see your cruelly handsome face dissolve into that of a blubbering infant when you get a mental image of a twenty-mile-high mushroom blotting out the friendly

Mediterranean sun, the Knesset Building burning like tinder, the bulk of your population incinerated, your organization and your M.—"

"You bastard!" Bond rose, but the gloating Nazi hammered a fist into his mouth and he fell back on the cot.

"Take him to the Buddha," Holzknicht said to the TUSH-ys on guard at the tent flap.

I've mucked it up good this time, Bond thought, as four sneering Nazis laid hands on him. *Kopy's given some shark the sexiest meal of his life; these butchers are cuffing me about as though I were some harmless puppy, and Eretz Israel will be gutted in forty minutes.*

"Herr Doktor!" A technician was racing toward the giant. "The personnel in Cave Delta have seized two more intruders."

Holzknicht spoke into the walkie-talkie. "Continue the countdown, Von Werner, but be prepared to halt it should conditions warrant. Hellmann," he said to the excited technician, "have them brought to me for interrogation. They may be friends of Bond."

The four hurled Bond savagely into the tent, his head banging the tent pole.

A minute passed. Then he heard the sound of female voices protesting to Holzknicht.

"Kopy! Go-Down!" he cried.

"Iz!"

"Mr. Bond!"

They were dragged kicking and screaming into the tent. Holzknicht, coldly furious, said, "Now, Miss Katz, I am in no mood for trifling. What were you doing in that cave? You were seen blown out to sea. And who is this Japanese woman?"

Bond glommed the two sets of fascinating protuberances and a cylinder in his mind began composing a song, "I'd Love To Be Strayin' Down Mammary Lane," but the other cylinder screamed: *Neck check! neck check!*

His eyes flew back to Kopy's silver AZK chain.

A thrill sped through him.

The plunger was gone.

25

Dem Bones, Dem Bones, Dem Dry Bones

Kopy's all too flimsy yarn of an urge to go spelunking with a friend made Holzknicht even angrier and he slapped her about viciously. Six Nazis had to sit on Bond to restrain him.

At last Holzknicht tired of pummeling the oval face and turned to Hellmann. "Were they carrying any sort of weapons, satchel charges, Calgonite time bombs?"

"*Nein, Herr Doktor,*" the man answered. "The guards spotted them almost immediately. Their feet hit one of the trip wires, setting off the alarm. All they had on them was"—he gave the two maidens a long, lascivious look—"all they have on them now."

"BO minus ten and counting, *Herr Doktor,*" Von Werner signaled.

"Very well," Holzknicht said. "It appears, Miss Katz, that your foray was unfruitful. Did you expect to upset my plans with those soft powerless hands? Take the *Juden* to the Buddha. I want the lovers to see my rapture when I learn of the detonation."

"And the one he calls Go-Down, *Herr Doktor?*"

"Kill her, Hellmann."

Go-Down Mikimoto spoke in her timid way. "May I kiss him *sayonara,* sir?"

"How poignant," smirked Holzknicht. "Love's last kiss. Be quick about it."

"*Domo arigato, Herr Doktor.* You are generous to your enemies." Go-Down Mikimoto knelt before Bond and kissed the swollen fingers. "Your poor dear hands, hands that have given me such delight. Would that I could free them from these cruel straps!" Then she rose and pressed her lips in longing against his sensual mouth. Her wriggling tongue forced his lips apart and he thought, *Why is she playing the* français *way?* —until he felt the small, sharp object slicing the inside of his cheek.

A *nakawari* shell! An Ama diving girl familiar with the creatures of her environment would, of course, have used such shells in the past to cut ropes, scrape barnacles from her dory, clean fish, etc.

"Good-bye, Mr. Bond." Her eyes flooded as Hellmann grasped her arm and dragged her off.

"Iz," said Kopy, choking on her own tears. "Don't look back."

A Luger roared twice.

Hellmann rejoined them, indifferently wiping blotches of claret from the front of his polo shirt. *"Ach,* so much blood for such a slight girl. I fear this shirt has been ruined permanently." When he saw Bond's jaw bulge, he kicked him in the leg. "Drive all thoughts of revenge from your mind, *Jude.* This is the end."

"BO minus two and counting," said the walkie-talkie in Holzknicht's hand.

Holzknicht held up his hand for the party to halt some three hundred yards from the Great Herrosukka Buddha. Even its impassive face seemed to hold a malicious grin. "Open Buddha."

There was a hissing sound and the Buddha began to divide. As the knees spread apart, there was the bird, slim and white, a swastika painted on its nuclear nose.

"With a phallus like that, no wonder you've been contemplating your navel," said an envious Bond to the deity. Now he felt the utter futility of their risible counterattack. Even if Kopy had put the stuff, whatever it was, into the bird, what possible effect could it have on this one-hundred-foot death-dealer?

"... three, two, one, zero. Ignition!"

Towering steam cumuli roiled out of the earth. The reverberation was deafening. Then the bird lifted off, slowly at first, but it gathered speed and soon was a pencil propelled by a dagger of flame.

Then it was out of sight.

"Auf Wiedersehen, Eretz Israel!" screamed Dr. Ernst Holzknicht, jumping up and down like a schoolboy. "TUSH has avenged *Der Führer!"*

Bond, whose face had been battered by rocks, branches and insects blown about in a dust storm whipped up by the lifting bird, knelt in a prayerful attitude.

Holzknicht laughed. "All the litany from the *Sh'ma Israel* to *Adon Olam* will not help now, *Jude*. The bird is on its way."

Bond *was* praying. But with his tongue tip he was also easing the *nakawari* shell out of the pouch in his right cheek, wincing again and again as the edge scored the sensual inner lining and his lower gum. He got the dull side between his teeth, craned his neck and began to work the sharp one against the saranoflex straps.

It was a long, laborious business. His mouth bled profusely, his head ached and as his jaw bumped his blackish hands, spears of pain ran up his arms.

Now some of the Nazis were coming back from the tent with chairs, a table, a two-way shortwave radio and some refreshments.

"Continue praying, Herr Bond," Holzknicht said. "It is good for the soul. If you like I shall teach you some hymns to Himmler. They would be far more appropriate at the moment."

Bond did not answer and the Nazi laughed again. "Miss Katz, join me in a stein of good Bavarian beer."

"With pleasure, *Herr Doktor,*" Kopy said gaily, walking toward the table in a sensual undulation that caused the other nine Nazis to gulp.

"You do not seem distressed at the day's developments," Holzknicht remarked, pouring the beer.

"*Herr Doktor,* I am a scientist also," said Kopy. "Political subdivisions mean nothing to me, nor do shopworn religions. My interest is in science, pure and simple. I have nothing but the greatest admiration for you and your colleagues. To think, you built a missile under Japan's nose!"

That's it, baby. Give me time, time! One strap is severed, but there are four more to go, Bond messaged her.

"Yet you are in love with this God-intoxicated broken vessel of a hero of your own heritage," Holzknicht said keenly.

"Was. And only for his once attractive body, which is not so any more. I admit I tried to save him by stealing in through the caves, but that was before I noticed so many fine German bodies."

A "Hear! hear!" erupted from the assemblage, who began to pound the table.

"Would you prove that, Miss Katz, by yielding to me before this wrecked Hebrew, so that he can see your exquisite pleasure?" Hellmann asked, squeezing his thighs together in his excitement.

"A charming proposal," said Kopy. "Herr Hellmann, you *are* a saucy rascal! Indeed I shall take you on. All of you. But should we not first experience the orgiastic moment of the missile's explosion. In a few minutes or so it will be crisping the sands of Egypt—"

Bond's head bobbed. Three more straps came apart.

"Egypt?" Holzknicht smiled humorlessly. "A joke, Miss Katz, and a poor one."

Kopy Katz stood up tall and proud. *"Herr Doktor..."*

Sit down, darling! Bond telepathed the Xeroxite. *You're overplaying your hand! For God's sake, sit down and button your adorable raspberry-float lips!*

The last strap was half severed. His eyes looked about for a weapon. There—there was something, jagged and bleached, near a *yoni* bush which had been set afire by the heat from the bird. It looked like one of the memorial bones that had been piled near the Buddha's base. It was!

Holzknicht, fiddling with the radio, said, "Go on, Miss Katz."

"You filthy, cold-blooded, murdering kraut!" The mask of levity fell off. "No, your boys didn't find anything on me in Cave Delta. I'd expected a trip-wire warning system, told Go-Down to kick one of them to set up a diversion, and while they were grabbing her I tossed a tiny quantity of a certain liquid into an open hatch on one of your tanks. Shall I give you the scientific formula, *Herr Doktor?*" She rattled off a long string of chemical terms totally incomprehensible to Bond, now crawling toward the burning bush.

Dr. Ernst Holzknicht's golden curls turned ash white. The pasty face began to drip soggy flesh.

"Gott in Himmler!" he screamed. He brought up his Luger, which seemed like a toy in the steam-shovel hand, and shot Kopy Katz in the head at pointblank range.

"Holzknicht, you bastard!"

Israel Bond, his makeshift bludgeon in his hand, sprang onto the table, sending Nazis flying head over heels.

"Die, Holzknicht, die!"

He swung the bleached object down, an incredible electric power surging through his right arm.

The TUSH leader's head exploded in saucer-sized fragments. Claret-soaked curls of golden fleece flew in every direction.

Thwack! Hellmann's hurried Luger shot thumped into Bond's left shoulder, but it was the bite of a mosquito.

Then Hellmann's skull was sundered by a blow from Bond, and Von Werner's, and another Nazi's, and another Nazi's....

One of their shots ripped his thigh, two more smacked into his right shoulder, a fourth creased his sensual scalp, but he steamrollered on and they began to scream in sheer terror, for he seemed to be framed in a golden aura, unafraid, unstoppable, unconquerable, his weapon smashing, crushing, battering, pulverizing....

Then the power was cut off and he fell like a great oak to the earth, the blood pouring out of him like the sea through a breached dike. Next to his ear was the radio, still squawking. "... *Herr Doktor,* something has gone wrong. It is many seconds past detonation time and we have seen nothing. Wait! Something evil comes this way! Something white and swift... something... *eeya-a-a-ah!*"

There was a protracted whine and the Egyptian end of the hookup went dead.

26
Now Heah de Wud
of de Lawd

Ten seconds after the *Kyodo Kikaku Kommando* choppers hit the cliff top, buzzing like great cicadas, Baron Cockimamiyama Sanka, a Hanyatti in one hand, a Cal-grenade dangling from his finger, gave a long, low whistle.

"By the belly of Buddha! This is a pocket-size Armageddon! Domo, tell the men to fan out and search. Kill anything that offers opposition."

Nothing did. From the caves came a bevy of Japanese workmen, their hands held high, their eyes fearful as they walked through a landscape of indescribable grue.

One by one the KKK began to stack up the bodies—the Nazis, many of whose heads were shapeless, splintered mounds, and the three dead women.

As Holzknicht's body was dumped on the heap by six sweating Kommandos, Sanka's mouth curled in a sneer and spat a wad of Copenhagen snuff onto the melted face. "Roast in hell!"

"Baron, we have found the Israeli," said Major Domo.

"*Yo-i!* Is he alive?"

"Barely. There is a stertorous rumbling in his chest. He is horribly wounded."

"Tell Dr. Spokko to come at once with plasma."

The pale secret agent lay still in a pool of claret, a strange peace on the cruelly handsome visage.

"That object he continues to clutch so tightly," said Major Domo. "It is blood-red. Apparently he used it as a club against his foes. But I have never before seen any bludgeon like it."

Sanka worked the long, tapering fingers out of the holes they had dug into the weapon. "Dr. Spokko, I suggest an immediate injection of adrenalin straight into the heart. It is the only hope."

"*Hai,*" nodded the doctor and prepared it. "Incidentally, my dear Baron and Major, from my considerable knowledge of the higher forms I should say unequivocally that the thing you took from the *gaijin's* hand is the jawbone of an ass."

27

How to Talk to a Jewish Mother

"*Herr Doktor* Ernst Holzknicht played the old shell game with Kopy Katz, and he lost," said Bond, his eyes on the horizon. Soon, he knew, three new ghosts, Kopy, Go-Down and Magma, would be forming out there to haunt him forevermore. Even Sarah Lawrence might decide to re-materialize. He wondered how they'd do it. En masse? In six-hour shifts?

"Explain that, Iz, darling," said Dr. Betty Freudan. "I'm not up on this missile-technology bit."

"In truth, she played the *new* shell game—Super Shell, to be precise. Lavi gave her the formula for Platformate, the ingredient that makes new Super Shell the world's greatest gasoline, and she put it into the hydrocarbon fuel. So powerful was the thrust of just that pinch of Platformate that the inertial-guidance system on the missile couldn't cope with it. The bird overshot Eretz Israel, as Lavi had computed, and nosed into central Egypt. Exeunt one missile base and only heaven knows how many Nazi scientists."

He lit a Raleigh and made a disquieting, though hardly earth-shaking, discovery.

He liked Raleigh cigarettes.

Funny, he ruminated, *maybe I always did. It was only a longing for status that made me snip away at the integrity of Raleigh with all the lousy, snotty jokes. I guess when you reach a certain level of maturity you finally discover what's real and right and true and what's dross. Dammit, I'd smoke Raleighs even if they* didn't *give coupons!*

"And it's worked out so neatly, dearest," trilled the lovely blond psychoanalyst. "Because they need Japanese trade so badly, Red China and Russia have denied they ever monitored the missile flight over their territories. Your pal Goshen of the

CIA has convinced the Tall Texan that the U.S. should stay mum, too. It's the biggest clam-up in history and the Cairo Colonel is being blamed for the detonation. He'll again be an international pariah for a long time and that can't hurt us. Darling, I think you've been out in the sun a flerm of a furge* too long. I'd better wheel you back into the kitchen."

He *was* tired. Maybe he was pushing the recovery bit a little too hard. It was only two weeks since he, kept clinically alive by the adrenalin shot and Major Domo's bottle of infection-fighting Excedrins, had been taken in Sanka's Lear jet to the Hadassah Medical Center near Jerusalem, where the real touch-and-go battle had been waged.

Eretz Israel's finest medicos had been rushed from an international convention on fee-splitting in Geneva to toil around the clock. They'd performed six open-heart massages, ten closed ones, and Lord knows how many tracheotomies, given him continual transfusions, even tried a daring innovation—the computer-driven electric *chrysteer*.**

It all seemed in vain the night his fever hit 112, but M., dipping into her bag of Hasidic medical lore, had brought it down to 110 by massive infusions of her chicken soup and the rarely used method known as *bankas*.*** Then she recalled an inspired remedy from her childhood in the Ukrainian village of Baronevkeh, from whence Bond's parents had come also. It was a Guggle Muggle, a mixture of boiling milk, honey, butter and schnapps. But M.'s was no run-of-the-mill Guggle Muggle. The milk came from Schleswig-Holsteins, the sassiest, most pampered cattle on God's green earth; the honey was manufactured under the strict supervision of Kosher queen bees in sterile hives built by the Levitt people; the butter was Breakstone's sweetest and creamiest; the schnapps from the cellar of Dean Martin. Even the glass had been blown from molten jade dust at the command of the grateful Emperor of Japan.

Seconds after he'd drunk it, his temperature fell to 98.6, thus enabling the surgeons to go to work on his body wounds, and the lead they extracted was sufficient for Lavi HaLavi to make Bond an ID bracelet.

---

*   The solar metric measurement of a pip of a popkin. One achieves it by adding dark matter to the speed of light.
**   Enema
***   Cupping

Betty wheeled him into the typical hubbub of the kitchen. "Let's have a little less hub and more bub," Bond said. A weak one-liner, he knew, but the hell with it! Even Jay Burton and Sheldon Keller have their off days.

M. alternated cooking and sending directives to Israeli agents everywhere, who'd be quietly disposing of the remaining TUSH small fry. Op Chief Lazar Beame banged away at his Smith-Corona on an article the *Reader's Digest* had asked him to submit: "Spies Can Be Good Neighbors and Solid Citizens, Too." Z., who'd just cracked a new Syrian code, got so excited he cracked the decoder as well.

And there was Neon Zion, 113, licensed to wound, ashamed to look Bond in the face as he whispered, "And I wanted your Oy Oy Seven number. I'm not fit to polish your bedsocks, Mr. Bond."

"Kid," Bond said tenderly, "you are. Go to it or I'll make a cripple from you, too."

His entrance was the signal for more broad smiles and affectionate words. *One thing I'll say for them,* he thought. *Whenever I come back from a job mutilated they appreciate it.*

"Oy Oy Seven, dear boy!"

It was Lavi HaLavi, dressed in a shepherd's tunic and buskins.

"Lavi!" Bond hugged the little genius to his heart, not caring about the pain. "Lavi, old chum. Your Xerox formula saved my life."

"I'm so happy, Oy Oy Seven. Everything's going splendidly today. My moon probe has just returned after taking samples of the lunar textures. Here, have a taste. It's superfab."

"Lavi, you expect me to eat that awful looking stuff?"

"My dear fellow, a good piece of green cheese never hurt anybody."

The 3-D signal—Danger! Doom! Disaster!—clanged from a large soup tureen on a top shelf.

The hilarity and high jinks stilled. That signal had oft rung before and everyone present knew what it meant.

Z. broke the stillness. "M., look at the two words that just came over the teletype."

The chipper old Number One ripped off the paper, read it, her face gaining ten new wrinkles, and passed it around to the other members of M 33 and 1/3.

It came to Bond last. And as he read the two coded words—
TITMOUSE TWEETER—he knew why. Without verbalizing, they
were asking him to take the job.

He searched each pair of eyes—Beame's, Z.'s, young Neon's,
Betty's and, of course, M.'s—and found the same plea: *Go in there,
Oy Oy Seven, and do what must he done.*

He closed his eyes and tried to imagine what TITMOUSE
TWEETER would be like. No, a job like that was beyond imagination. He did know what was in store: hot lead would lay open his
shoulders, loathsome hirsute things that lurked in the humid
Amazon night would sink their fangs into his thighs; his cruelly
handsome face would feel the knout, the brass knuckle, the
truncheon, the stiffened, calloused fingers of the killer karateist.
And my eyes ... and incidentally, are they *gray* or *grey*? Who cares?

Israel Bond rose haltingly from the wheelchair and took a
few unsteady steps toward M., the woman to whom he gave his
total love and trust.

He ran his long, tapering fingers over her peruke and
let them steal down her tabescent cheeks and she smiled her
maternal, heart-catching smile.

Quietly and with the heartwarming grin that made him the
consummate human being the world had come to adore, he said
in a tender tone:

"Fuck it."

He flipped his Double-Oy gold-edged security card to Neon
Zion and told the lad, "Go kill and be well." He turned at the door
and said in Yiddish:

"Genig iz shen genig. A mann darft leben. Enough is enough
already ...a man needs to live."

He strode out of the dark kitchen into the sunshine of Jerusalem and in seven seconds was lost in the crowd.

Epis-A-logue

The moving finger, having writ, falls off.
SOL WEINSTEIN
Tokyo and Atami, Japan, 1966.
Levittown, Pa., 1967.
Unemployment and Panic, 1968.

About the Author

We asked Sol Weinstein, author of the Hebrew Secret Agent Israel Bond (Oy Oy Seven) thrillers to describe his fulsome career in three sentences. They are: 1 1/2 – 3 months for kiting checks ... 2 1/2 months for illegally checking kites at a Tokyo kids' fair ... and 1 week for pushing Stepan Novotny, infamous forger, from the top of the Prague National Bank. (The Czech bounced.)

In addition to Oy Oy Seven's capers in *Loxfinger, Matzohball, On the Secret Service of His Majesty the Queen,* and *You Only Live Until You Die*, he wrote a highly sentimental set of music and lyrics to "The Curtain Falls", sung by Kevin Spacey in the biopic *Beyond the Sea* in his role as Bobby Darin.

Sol currently resides in New Zealand, is a member of Temple Sinai in Wellington, and pronounces a favourite ethnic food as "kiegel", not "kugel".

If you enjoyed this book...

...or if you enjoy getting books that you don't enjoy, then look for the full run of Israel Bond Oy-Oy-7 books wherever you got this book. (Unless you found it on a bus or something, because, really, what are the odds of repeating that sort of stroke of amazingly good luck?)

Also available for the Kindle, the Nook, the iPad, and other electronic devices.

Oy-Oy-7.com

www.ingramcontent.com/pod-product-compliance
Lightning Source LLC
LaVergne TN
LVHW011332080426
835513LV00006B/296